A CIVIC TECHNOLOGIST'S PRACTICE GUIDE

BY CYD HARRELL

A Civic Technologist's Practice Guide
by Cyd Harrell

Five Seven Five Books
San Francisco, California
a personal imprint

Please report errors at cydharrell.com

Author and Publisher: Cyd Harrell
Editor: Sally Kerrigan
Cover and Interior Design: Oxide Design
Copy Editor: Caren Litherland

for everyone doing the work

TABLE OF CONTENTS

Introduction   **11**

Chapter 1: What Is Civic Tech?   **17**
- Government in the United States: It's Complicated   19
- What Does Tech Have to Offer Here?   23
- Navigating a Nebulous Problem Space   24
- Public Servants as Stakeholders and Colleagues   26

Chapter 2: Reckoning with Privilege   **29**
- Tech and the Privilege of Credibility   30
- Undoing the Tech Savior Complex   32
- Representation and Privilege in Civic Tech Work   33
- Making Civic Tech for Everyone   35
- Being an Ally   36

Chapter 3: Ways to Contribute   **39**
- Stepping Forward: Volunteer Collaborations   40
- The Business of Government Tech: Startups and Other Vendors   42
- Going All In: Innovation Labs and Digital Service Teams   43
- For the People, by the People: Citizen Engagement and Mutual Aid   45
- Making Partnerships and Spaces Inclusive   46

Chapter 4: Project Types   **49**
- Service Delivery Projects   50
- Infrastructure and Data Projects   51
- Specialized Tools for Digital Government   54
- Swooping In for a Rescue   55

Chapter 5: Innovation and Its Discontents   **59**
- Innovation Is a Flawed Framework for Change   60
- Bureaucracy and Stewardship   62
- Perspectives on Risk and Failure   64
- The Role of Prototypes   65
- Digital Transformation and Continuous Improvement   66

Chapter 6: Working in Regulated Spaces   69

- Budgets, Cycles, and Procurement   70
- Regulations and Tooling   73
- How Long Does All This Take?   75
- Becoming Part of the Relay   78

Chapter 7: Essential Skills   79

- What Skills Do You Need to Succeed in Civic Tech?   80
- Know Your Limits: Levels of Competence   81
- Frameworks and Flexibility   83
- Not-Strictly-Tech Work in Civic Tech   85
- If You're Starting Your Career   86

Chapter 8: Project Teams and Methods   89

- Government Teams and Assumptions   90
- Open-Source Teams and Assumptions   91
- The Engineering-Design-Product Triad   92
- Leveling Up Partner Teams   93
- Filling in for Product Management   95

Chapter 9: Working with Policy   97

- How Policy Evolves in Practice   98
- Policy Implementation Is the Biggest Opportunity for Tech   100
- How Can Tech Methods Apply?   102
- Technology Policy   104
- Policy Exceptions and Change   105

Chapter 10: Making Long-Term Change   107

- Open Data   108
- Improving Procurement   109
- Legacy Migrations   111
- Metrics and Analytics   112
- User-Centered Design   113
- Bringing Capabilities Inside   115
- Moving Traditional Entities Forward   116

Chapter 11: Harmonizing Ways of Working 119

- Work Culture: Tech versus Government 120
- Your Jargon, My Jargon 122
- Techniques of Professional Inclusion 123
- Rigidity and Hierarchy 124

Chapter 12: The Allies We Need 127

- Executive Champions and Strategic Alignment 128
- Mid-Level, Socially Connected Partners 129
- Legal and Regulatory Colleagues 131
- Partners from Outside Government 132
- Communications and the Press 134

Chapter 13: Pace, Risks, and Self-Care 137

- Rotations, Terms, and the Long Term 138
- Pacing Yourself 139
- The Logistics Burden 141
- Financial Risks and Planning 142
- How to Recognize Burnout 143
- Cultivating the Karass 145

Conclusion 149

Resources 151

Further Reading 157

Acknowledgments 163

About the Author 167

INTRODUCTION

Welcome to *A Civic Technologist's Practice Guide.* Whether you've been at this for fifteen years or are just now contemplating a career shift, I want to thank you for thinking about how (and if) technology can make civic life better.

How technologists think about and go about their practice is an important factor in whether tech is a force for good, a force for ill, or completely irrelevant. As the field matures, our responsibilities grow; what began as a volunteer-run "civic hacking" weekend event might now be someone's full-time charge in a Digital Innovation office. The opportunities are enormous, and we need many more civic technologists—especially Black and brown techies and others from currently under-represented backgrounds—to bring these opportunities to fruition.

I entered civic tech as a full-time career in 2012, after a couple years of experimenting with volunteer efforts and trying to find my role. I'm a UX researcher, and when I started going to hackathons, I wasn't sure if there was room for people from the design world at all. There certainly weren't many recognizable design roles in government. But I badly wanted to contribute my skills to the public good, so I started showing up at weekend events and offering to help. The projects were fascinating and, somewhat to my surprise, nobody ever sent me home because I couldn't code.

When Code for America (CfA) was founded, its office happened to be just two blocks from mine in San Francisco, so I reached out to Jennifer Pahlka and asked if I could mentor their fellows in research. I had never experienced such rewarding work, and when the little research company I worked for was sold to Facebook in 2012, I knew it was time for a career shift. It took me six months to convince CfA to hire me, and in the interim I got to help Dana Chisnell research one of the *Field Guides to Ensuring Voter Intent*.[1] More than anyone else in the field, I've been influenced by Dana's practice, especially the time and care she and her colleagues put into building relationships with election officials.

Over the past eight years, I've seen success, failure, and a lot of ambiguity. I've become well-known in the field, but I share my meandering path for anyone who isn't sure there's a place for them in civic tech. I'll say it loud: if you have *any* technology skill that is strong enough to teach someone else, then there's good work you can do and we'd love to have you.

I talk every week with people who hope to use their hard-earned technology skills to make the world a better place, many of them disillusioned about the potential of private-sector tech to do so. I also talk with colleagues who are deep into their civic tech careers—elated by a success, exhausted by a failure, facing a new dilemma. Disillusionment and overwhelm are natural in jobs like ours, given that our project in US civic tech aims to change foundational institutions that have existed for hundreds of years. Institutional change is political by definition; we're trying to shift the relationships of major, society-sustaining entities to their constituents

Is technology the way to solve these problems? It's an urgent question for the 2020s and beyond. I believe that technology *can* make civic life

---

1 The *Field Guides* are very short guides to all aspects of election design, from ballots to signage. Center for Civic Design, *Field Guides to Ensuring Voter Intent*, https://civicdesign.org/fieldguides/.

better, but that it often fails to do so—sometimes catastrophically and with real harm.

Because we are so new on the scene, and the institutions we seek to change are so large and impact so many lives, each of us needs to be conscious of our values and assumptions. We need to be able to explain ourselves to partners and stakeholders, and to be able to regularly check whether we are truly doing good. In my own approach to civic tech (and in this book), I assume several foundational elements are important:

- collaborative workstyles
- iterative, evidence-based practice, whether in development, design, or policy
- user-centered design
- secure and sustainable technology
- public transparency and accountability
- full participation in civic life and civic tech by people from underrepresented groups

This book, written as civic tech enters its teenage years, aims to gather together some of the most useful principles and practices for institutional work that have emerged so far.

Because the field is new, and operating at the intersection of very different working cultures, you will be comparatively alone and in charge of organizing your own work on most civic tech projects, no matter your professional level. Even if you join an established team, each new engagement will bring questions of how best to partner, and how to shape a project for the biggest impact at each stage. Many chapters in this book are intended to help think through these questions.

I assume you already have improvements you want to make or specific people you want to serve; choosing one of those is a personal question that goes beyond the scope of this book. To achieve your goals in civic tech, you'll need to figure out:

- which part of the ecosystem you need to work in to affect it (Chapter 1)
- which style of partnership suits your situation best (Chapter 3)
- which kind of project will have the biggest impact (Chapter 4)
- how to apply your specific skill set and what additional skills you may need (Chapter 7)
- how to ensure your efforts last (Chapter 10)

And there's much more to working in the civic space successfully and sustainably. *How* we work affects how much good we do and how long we're able to keep it up. So other chapters cover:

- taking account of our privilege both as technologists and, for many of us, as people benefiting from racial or other privileges (Chapter 2)
- wrestling with the idea of innovation and what it means to the field (Chapter 5)
- learning what to expect when working in spaces with major constraints (Chapter 6)
- considering team structures and methods for public-sector work (Chapter 8)
- discovering what civic technologists need to know about public policy (Chapter 9)
- learning how to bridge tech and government working cultures (Chapter 11)
- identifying allies at all levels and building partnerships with them (Chapter 12)
- taking care of ourselves along the way (Chapter 13)

Because its goal is change, civic tech embodies an interesting split between demonstrating and operationalizing the potential of modern tech. I like to call these two branches *showing what's possible* and *doing what's necessary*. Many projects are a mix of the two, but they require different mindsets. "Showing what's possible" is about speed, prototyping, design, public feedback, and data. These are often web projects because web tools are great for those purposes. "Doing what's necessary," on the other hand, is about shifting the underlying practices and systems: back-end systems, security, and procurement; hiring and team composition; even shifting budget priorities.

In this book, I've intentionally focused more on principles, categories, and sets of questions than on explicit methodology. I don't think it matters much whether you decide to use Scrum on your project, but I do think that the principles of iterative development are essential and you should consider the most suitable way to make them part of your and your partners' shared practice. I don't know which strategic framework will work best for your situation, but I do know that if you don't form strong partnerships with career staff and stakeholders, your efforts will fail.

The private-sector tech industry focuses on scale a great deal, but public institutions represent a different kind of scale. They affect people's lives not just at enormous breadth, but over long stretches of time. Most of them operate in full awareness of this, seeing their role as one of stewardship of public goods (and public funds) rather than rapid innovation.

With this different perspective on scale and time, we technologists have to earn our way to working on deeper layers of digital public infrastructure through steady and trustworthy partnership on surface-level projects. Whether we're developers, designers, data people, or product managers, we often do our most effective work by focusing on small changes at deeper infrastructural layers of whatever "stack" we work on. My goal with this book is to set you up for success and get you to that level of practice.

Across the thousands of entities and cultures that make up the American civic sphere, there's no one place to look for answers to the questions each of us faces about where and how to do this work—and so I hope that this book will serve as an anchor for a conversation that, as we are about to enter our teenage years as a field, is coming due.

CHAPTER 1
WHAT IS CIVIC TECH?

I subscribe to the definition that government is *what we do together.* Working in civic technology means partnering with any of thousands of entities in the wide universe of civic institutions, all with the common goal of improving public life. Between the federal government, the fifty state governments, the approximately three thousand county-level governments, and the municipal governments of over twenty thousand cities and towns, there are close to twenty-five thousand entities in the United States' civic sphere—and that doesn't even count tribal governments and regional districts that don't map to city or county boundaries. Add on community organizations that also serve the public, and we're looking at tens of thousands of possible partners.

Civic tech is a loosely integrated movement that brings the strengths of the private-sector tech world (its people, methods, or actual technology) to public entities with the aim of making government more responsive, efficient, modern, and more just. It also seeks to use digital tech to reimagine interactions among fellow citizens[1] working together, and between those citizens and their governments.

Simply put, those of us who work in civic tech want public digital goods to be as good as the ones made by commercial entities like Apple or Google—and we want public digital infrastructure[2] to be as good, too. We want to access services, exercise rights, and build communities with the ease and respect that the best digital technology can afford.

Tall order.

And because it is such a tall order, I like to think of civic tech as a fifty-year project, with the start of the timeline around 2008. That summer, the city of Washington, DC, hosted an Apps for Democracy hackathon that kick-started the city-focused and largely volunteer-driven open data movement. By the time the Code for America Brigade launched in 2012, the movement was active in over twenty cities, and lower-profile initiatives had begun percolating throughout the federal government as well.

These early initiatives introduced an optimistic view of what government could be, an eagerness to act rather than just publish, and an ability to attract people who might not have considered working in the public sector before. It's worth noting that all of these early organizations were founded and led by people with a lot of power in our existing system. None of these initiatives was truly diverse in the beginning, and the problems stemming from this persist in the field to this day.

Civic tech, in its fifty-year timeline, is now in its adolescence—which means it's the right time to reckon with the way power is distributed within the movement. While many individuals and institutions have contributed to the development of civic tech, most of its culture comes

---

1 I'm using the term *citizen* carefully here, with awareness that a person's formal national citizenship status affects their relationship with some levels of government profoundly and others much less so. "Resident" and "constituent", which I use elsewhere, don't have the same connotation of active, empowered participation.

2 Ethan Zuckerman outlined this idea in a January 2020 blog post for the Knight First Amendment Institute at Columbia University. See Zuckerman, "The Case for Digital Public Infrastructure," Knight First Amendment Institute, January 17, 2020, https://knightcolumbia. org/content/the-case-for-digital-public-infrastructure.

from a few early centers that were operating in the early 2010s,[3] before the US national teams came into being. The field is still shaped by a large number of alumni from these groups, with strong perspectives.

Civic tech in 2020 is a complicated, imperfect field that comprises multiple national, state, and city teams, a vast network of volunteer networks, an infrastructure of major non-profit funders, and a growing ecosystem of companies large and small—to say nothing of tens of thousands of individuals. I urge you to approach it with both an open mind and a skeptical attitude, and to see yourself as a part of it from your very first steps, with the power to change it for the better.

GOVERNMENT IN THE UNITED STATES: IT'S COMPLICATED

As a civic technologist, a basic understanding of the American government will help you figure out how to work effectively within and across various branches and entities that have complex relationships with one another. Residents of the United States need to interact with all of the four major levels of government: federal, state, county, and municipal. Each level replicates, more or less, the three-branch structure of executive, legislative, and judiciary: you'll find elected legislatures, executive branches headed by elected leaders and administered by permanent staff, and court systems run by appointed or elected judges.

There are some exceptions to the rule. Not all states have municipal-level courts, and not every town has one even where they do; quite a few large cities have "unified" city/county governments (like Miami-Dade County or the City and County of San Francisco); and this leaves out sovereign tribes and governing bodies that don't map neatly onto the geographical categories (often park or resource districts).

---

3 For my money, the most culturally influential civic tech institutions are Code for America, the Sunlight Foundation, the HealthCare.gov rescue team (which supplied many early US Digital Service staffers), and the early teams at the Consumer Financial Protection Bureau.

With some overlap and cooperation, the branches within each level are responsible for different civic functions. This table lists just a few of each level's functions that members of the public interact with directly.

BRANCH	EXECUTIVE	LEGISLATIVE	JUDICIARY
Federal	**The President** **Cabinet agencies and independent agencies** • Collect federal income taxes • Oversee immigration and passports • Fund major benefits programs; administer Social Security • Oversee veterans' services • Make regulations • Manage national Parks	**Senate** **House of Representatives** • Pass laws (which supersede and constrain state laws) • Oversee the federal budget, including setting income and business tax rates	**Supreme Court** • decides appeals from other federal courts or state supreme courts **Federal district and appeals courts** • deal with federal crimes, immigration, bankruptcy
State	**Governor** **State cabinet agencies** • Voter registration • Driver and vehicle licensing • State income taxes • Business registration • Professional licensing • State Parks • Fishing and hunting licenses • Highway patrol	**One or two-house state legislature** • Pass laws (if these contradict federal law that can generate a Supreme Court case) • Administer state budget • Set state income and/or sales taxes	**State supreme court** **State courts of appeals** • Some states have separate lower courts for family law
County	**County executive** • Sheriffs • Birth, death, and marriage records • Administration of state programs • Election administration (mostly) • Transit and roads • Parks	**County Council or Board of Supervisors** • County budget • Local statutes concerning land use, property matters, and alcohol sales (for example)	**Superior courts** (technically part of state court systems) • Most felonies must be tried in superior court • Many family law matters and minor lawsuits are handled here

BRANCH	EXECUTIVE	LEGISLATIVE	JUDICIARY
City or Town	**Mayor,** sometimes sharing power with an appointed City Manager • Local police • Building permitting • Parking and traffic • Parks • Schools (usually with a separate elected board) • Libraries	**City Council** • City budget • Local ordinances • Local property and sales taxes	**Municipal courts** (but not everywhere) • Misdemeanor offenses and infractions like traffic tickets

Resource levels vary hugely between and within levels. In the US, only about three hundred cities have a population of more than a hundred thousand. As you might expect, such cities have much more capacity to hire staff and buy technology products than smaller cities do, but there really isn't much difference between the variety of services a city of four hundred thousand needs to offer to the public and what a city of forty thousand needs to do on a much smaller budget. And collaborating nationwide across forty-thousand-person cities, which might seem like an obvious solution, isn't easy.

Cities offer an expectation of frequent contact with constituents across departments, which means much easier access to officials. They have smaller budgets, but it is often easier to create pilot programs or find exceptions to existing constraints. Accepting volunteer or pro bono services from the public is generally okay, at least in the short term. Cities' smaller size also means that after some work, you might be able to convene a meeting of key decision-makers in one room. This makes it possible to move faster and more nimbly, even if at a smaller scale.

The United States federal government is in a class of its own as a large institution, employing almost three million people (if you include the armed services) and with a multitrillion dollar yearly budget. Many government employees refer to it as *the* government, and it's possible to plan and execute entire careers within the federal space. It is large enough to have its own ecosystem of technology publications, conferences, and societies that barely intersects with its private-sector counterpart.

The federal government cannot accept labor from volunteers except in very narrow and extreme cases[4]. If you want to work on a tech matter at the federal level, your choices are basically to join up as an employee, get involved with advocacy groups pushing for the change you want, or get yourself appointed to some kind of commission. All of these are good options, but they're very different from how you would work with local-level partners.

States and counties fit somewhere in between these ends of the spectrum. They vary enormously in size, history, and political culture and have important responsibilities like registering voters, administering programs, and licensing (drivers and vehicles, but also doctors and lawyers). If you're here to fix the DMV, this is the level that handles it, and it's a very knotty problem indeed.

Most states and many counties are large enough that a relationship with a particular agency makes more sense than with the top-level executive, although a few states have recently established digital teams that serve other parts of the government. States and counties have budgets and often hiring mechanisms to bring in individual consultants or small firms (although there will be plenty of paperwork involved). Personal or organizational connections are going to matter a great deal at these levels compared to city-level work: every city has a city hall (and most have a website) that expects visits from constituents, but states and counties typically are less directly open. Working with someone, or a group, that understands the lay of the land is a very good idea.

INTERNATIONAL ROOTS OF CIVIC TECH

While this book is specifically about American civic tech, I want to point out a few important international antecedents. We should all remember that civic tech did not start in the US.

---

4 Like many things in government, this is for a good reason—the Antideficiency Act keeps agencies from committing taxpayer money before Congress votes on it, and also prevents the government from coming close to using slave labor in any way, shape, or form.

The UK's Government Digital Service (GDS) preceded the US Digital Service (USDS) by two years and established many of the principles civic technologists think of as important. USDS's Playbook unabashedly adopts several pieces of GDS's Design Principles and Service Manual.

Estonia, while much smaller in population, has invested in a largely digital national government since 2003, with 99 percent of government services available online as of 2020.

Even the US Web Design System was not the first national-government design system on our own continent. The Canadian Federal Government launched the Web Experience Toolkit/Boîte-Outils Expérience Web in 2012 and you can find it updated on Github to this day.

WHAT DOES TECH HAVE TO OFFER HERE?

The civic technology field comprises a broad network of interconnected groups and interests. Of the three major enablers of civic tech's ascendance, one is the insight that the principles of the Freedom of Information Act (FOIA) can also apply to government-produced *data*. The Freedom of Information Act is a broad directive requiring federal government-created information to be made public on request, unless there are specific reasons not to. There are similar laws in almost all state and local governments. In 2007, Tim O'Reilly and Carl Malamud convened a group that proposed adapting the same principle to requests for government datasets. The principle that government data belongs to the public and should be available for the public to review and work with became known as *open data*.

This was partly by analogy to *open-source software*, which had existed since the 1980s. Open source is a complex movement, but the core philosophy that matters to government tech is that software created collaboratively by many people, in public, is more robust than software developed privately. But how governments should license their code, and whether the public could contribute, didn't become major questions until the rise of platforms like GitHub offered easier ways to do so. This raised the second major enabling point that civic technologists pushed on in the early days: if all government publications are in the public domain by default, shouldn't all government-produced code be open-source by default and allow for public review and contribution?

While open-data advocates pushed for these ideas, the private sector cemented the dominance of the web as a customer service medium[5]— the third major enabler for civic tech, and one that weighs heavily in our conception of government services being for the people. The web's direct interface between customers and systems gave companies more immediate information about needs and desires, while its relative ease of change (compared to, say, physical retail environments or hard-wired mainframe systems) allowed quicker responses. This resulted in faster cycles of data and response—and, when things went well, it offered better service, greater satisfaction, and higher profits.

This is all great on the surface: more accountability and better service, thanks to civic tech. Sign me up, right? But of course, it's not that simple.

NAVIGATING A NEBULOUS PROBLEM SPACE

One of the real challenges of this multilayered government system is figuring out how to deliver improvements at a scale that will make the best use of your efforts. There is nothing wrong with simply starting local and pursuing collaboration with local agencies (in fact it's a great way to actually get something done, which may then have potential for reuse), but if your aim is to make a difference in the public's relationship with institutions, scale is probably on your mind. And it's a tough challenge for ambitious civic technology. Available scale is often in conflict with how directly you can see or measure outcomes.

---

5 Paul Ford made this point definitively in 2011. See Ford, "The Web Is a Customer Service Medium," Ftrain.com, January 6, 2011, https://www.ftrain.com/wwic.

Let's look at an example: public food assistance. It would be great if people who need food aid could get it more easily, and maybe there's a role for technology to play. If you want to develop a well-grounded hypothesis for how technology can help, and build a prototype, it will be really helpful to understand the complex system around food assistance:

- The Supplemental Nutrition Assistance Program (SNAP, a.k.a. food stamps) is funded through a congressional appropriation to the Department of Agriculture, which is then disbursed to the states in grants with stringent program and data requirements.
- The states set policies, and in some cases run the programs. In many states, though, the frontline SNAP administration, which determines benefit eligibility and gives people Electronic Benefits Transfer (EBT) cards to buy food with, is staffed by county-level officials, often in a Public Health department.
- On top of that, many people access benefits with help from a non-governmental organization (NGO).
- Those NGOs may in turn receive money from donors or local governments to fund their activities.

This landscape isn't exactly hidden, but it's not the first thing that stares practitioners in the face when they decide they want to do tech work for good. Which level offers the best opportunity to work on the problem you want, with the tools you have?

For public food-assistance projects, the federal level would offer mostly data and reporting work, while the state and county levels would likely offer multiple levels of design and development work. Some would be direct interfaces for the public; others would be more in the legacy migration or API arena.[6] NGOs in the space will also have a lot of information about the policies of the relevant agencies at each level, which can help when considering where partnerships would be useful and what you can add to the work already being done.

---

6 In the vast majority of cases, the existing systems will have been built by vendors, and you can find out about *them* by searching for news stories and RFPs.

PUBLIC SERVANTS AS STAKEHOLDERS AND COLLEAGUES

People who work in the private-sector tech industry, with its emphasis on passion demonstrated through long hours and side projects, are sometimes dismissive of "by-the-book" government staff. This is a mistake. After eight years of working exclusively in the civic field, I can tell you that the most rewarding part has been meeting people who chose public service lives and helping them use tech practices to further their missions. But there are things I wish I'd understood much earlier, starting with the different ways people become part of a government.

To use some federal jargon, there are *electeds*, *appointeds*, and *careers*. "Electeds" are directly accountable to voters, and it's fairly unusual for them to make better technology part of a campaign platform. But they can be high-profile champions of tech (many mayors, a few governors, and President Obama have been) or major channels of oversight in the case of elected legislators.

"Appointeds", as their name suggests, are appointed by elected leaders, often but not always as part of the elected leader's administration[7]. Appointed people often serve in leadership roles for agencies or departments, or in key internal oversight roles in the executive branch. They set direction for their areas of responsibility, and it has become very common for some technology leadership roles to be in this category. If your city or state has a Chief Digital Officer, a Chief Data Officer, or a Chief Technology Officer, or your state has a head of an office of technology or innovation, that is almost certainly an appointed role.

Appointed leaders are generally chosen for both their subject-matter expertise and their alignment with a given elected leader's priorities. Together with elected executives, they make up "the administration." If you are going to work with government agencies, be aware of the priorities of your current administration with respect to both technology and the mission areas you want to work in. If a change of administration

---

7 Judges and certain high-level commissions are the exception—someone can be appointed but their term is expected to outlast the leader who appointed them. However, there are many places in the US where judges are elected, usually in nonpartisan contests.

may be coming, consider what effect a change in priorities may have on your collaboration with that agency.

"Career" staff are the backbone of every agency, legislative office, and court. They do the bulk of the work involved in running these offices, and their presence smooths out transitions between elected administrations, keeps long-term initiatives on track, and provides nearly all of the direct services the government offers the public. They have—they *are*—institutional memory. These people have chosen public service as something they will do for perhaps several decades.

There's an important distinction in career government jobs between program staff and support staff, especially with contracting or IT positions. Technology is virtually always considered a support function, not a primary function, in government. Program staff perform services, spend and account for budgets, and communicate with constituents, while IT staff are charged with implementing technology programs. We'll dig into the nuances of roles and procurement in later chapters, but it's important to understand from the start that creating a bridge between IT and program staff will be required in almost every civic technologist's job.

Career staff often see their role in terms of stewardship—care and sustainment—of public funds and public functions. Those with long tenure can tell you why what you want to do failed the last time, and the time before that. They're critical allies and colleagues who have as much to contribute to civic technology work as you do.

• • •

With the right partners, your work in civic tech can help groups trying to address inequities and improve services in a huge variety of areas; as we've covered, the universe of government services is immense in the United States, and its problems are many. We have an opportunity in this field to use tech for good, not just for profit.

As you go about your work in civic tech, keep in mind the various levels and branches, and the ecosystem of players within and outside them. Do the work to understand the landscape in the area you're interested in. Look for places where policy favors the outcomes you want to see in the world, and where you have a path to partnership with core institutional stakeholders. Stewardship will always be part of the calculations governments make in deciding how to act. Bring it into yours as well, as a first step in meeting the civic world where it is.

CHAPTER 2
RECKONING WITH PRIVILEGE

Government in the United States has never been truly equitable, and neither has tech. Civic tech, being a bridge between these two arenas, suffers from many of the same structural inequities. As a field in its adolescence, however, it's in a unique position to address the inequities head-on before the same exclusionary habits calcify into a new area of practice. I couldn't write this book without discussing the civic tech field's history of exclusion and how we can become better.

Early volunteer civic tech efforts reflected the demographics of people who had the time and means to do free work, and in particular skewed toward engineers and open-source contributors. All of these categories tend to be whiter, more male, and more affluent than American society at large—and for a field that aspires to make technology for everyone, this is a problem.

Every civic tech space should be inclusive as well as diverse. Diversity refers to the representation of different types of people in a team or process, but inclusion goes further, recognizing that representation alone doesn't mean that the less privileged people on a team are well supported. Inclusive spaces don't just allow all people to participate, but actively value their differences and support them with what they need to participate fully.

The good news is that we're already beginning to see civic tech shift along these lines. One of the great strengths of the field as of 2020 is that more and more people from all kinds of backgrounds are joining it, partly due to inclusive recruiting initiatives at major civic tech organizations. Recent joiners bring with them a wealth of perspectives, skills, and experiences. But there's more we can do to keep that momentum going and to continue learning and improving.

TECH AND THE PRIVILEGE OF CREDIBILITY

There are far more men and far fewer Black and brown people in the makeup of tech companies than there would be if those companies reflected the population. Many of the women and people of color present are in support roles, or not in engineering.[1] The lack of diversity is a problem for an industry as influential as tech, but it's even more of a problem when technologists enter government institutions that need to serve the entire population.

When technologists walk into the conversation in civic tech settings, they enjoy some degree of automatic credibility. Decision-makers in government are predisposed to be impressed by the "new perspective," and may divert speaking time from any career civil servants in the room. It's true that the technological perspective can be incredibly useful to help resolve system-level quagmires in government (or anywhere, for that matter). But our job as civic technologists isn't to be the hero of the stories we stumble into halfway through; it's to understand and support

---

1 The Equal Employment Opportunity Commission (EEOC) reported on high tech industry demographics in 2014. See US Equal Employment Opportunity Commission, "Diversity in High Tech," 2014, https://www.eeoc.gov/special-report/diversity-high-tech. Since then, major tech companies have begun reporting their statistics yearly. See Sara Harrison, "Five Years of Tech Diversity Reports—and Little Progress," Wired, October 1, 2019, https://www.wired.com/story/five-years-tech-diversity-reports-little-progress/. The stats tell a frustrating tale of exclusion.

the people who have already been in place doing the work, and who want to use tech to make improvements.

And if most technologists are White or Asian men (even though those categories don't make up a majority of the population), then people unconsciously assume that a technologist looks like that, and people who match that assumption get double automatic credibility. On top of that, their perspectives, including the comfort that comes with automatic credibility, shape the entire industry because other perspectives are less likely to be strongly heard.

This automatic credibility is a form of *privilege*. Put most simply, someone with privilege has an unearned advantage that some people in a situation have and others don't. Privilege can skew the dynamics of a group of colleagues working together, even if some people (usually the privileged ones) aren't aware of it.

Thinking about privilege can be as painful and personal as it is necessary—not to mention confusing, because tech isn't *categorically* bad. Throughout the United States, the tech industry is associated with hard work, ingenuity, and smarts. People who work in tech tend to be fluent with technology and feel empowered to work with it. But there's a tendency to equate being "good at technology" with being "a smart person"—and it's easy to lose sight of the fact that these are *learnable* skills, which some people have more time than others to learn because of privilege.

It's an accident of history that makes tech skills and interests so publicly valued at this particular time; don't let it convince you that it makes techies any smarter than anyone else. Take your privilege into account as you do the work, and consider what you can learn from people who don't have the same technology background. If you're getting more attention from the people at the top, you can use that to make sure that others' perspectives are heard, too. You can also assume that your tech skills are teachable—not with the attitude that they're more important than other ways of working, but with humility and a willingness to share the credibility that comes from having them.

Understanding this will help you form effective partnerships founded on strong mutual respect. Better yet, the software that comes from a team like that is far more likely to meet people's needs.

UNDOING THE TECH SAVIOR COMPLEX

One particularly noxious form of privilege often seen in civic tech crops up when overrepresented people find out about a space where good can be done and enthusiastically jump in, assuming that they are the first to engage with it. This is almost never the reality. But, because of their privilege, this brand-new group may get all kinds of opportunities that were not available to the people already working on the issue. Intervention by an overrepresented group risks erasing those people, who are often the ones most directly impacted by the issue.

For example, in 2014, well-known venture capitalist Sean Parker launched Brigade, a citizen-engagement app with the not-at-all-novel mission of "making civic engagement easy, effective, and enjoyable." Multiple apps and companies already existed in the space,[2] and Horace Williams, a Black founder, was already working on what would become Empowrd, which launched in 2015. Furthermore, Code for America had launched its civic tech volunteer network, called the Brigade, in 2012.

Parker's launch took the civic tech community by surprise, but gained enormous mainstream press attention. It eventually disappeared through a maze of acquihires[3] without causing any significant change in the civic sphere, but it sufficiently distracted attention from the other groups working in the same space.

As it turns out, people working on challenging social issues are often members of underrepresented communities. Taking oxygen from their efforts isn't fair or right for many reasons. One of the simplest ways you

---

2 POPVOX, TurboVote, MindMixer, and Textizen, to name a few that are still operating in 2020.

3 *TechCrunch* covered most of the story in 2019. The engineering team ended up going to Pinterest. John Constine, "Sean Parker's Brigade/Causes Acquired by Govtech App Countable," *TechCrunch*, May 1, 2019, https://techcrunch.com/2019/05/01/brigade-countable/.

can avoid letting your privilege erase others is to check who is doing the work now. Because someone is. They may or may not look like a stereotypical tech group, but whoever they are, they have invaluable knowledge.

If you think of your job as using your tech skills to help give superpowers to people already doing the work and to amplify their impact, you will go wrong much less often. Our whole civic tech community must support projects led by underrepresented community members and public servants.

REPRESENTATION AND PRIVILEGE IN CIVIC TECH WORK

A diverse team is imperative to the success of any civic project that aims to serve a diverse community. People design for themselves by default—and people who are already overrepresented and accustomed to being in spaces where their group dominates may not even notice their own overrepresentation, or the harm this can produce at scale.

There are many axes of privilege that impact the way you experience the world. Consider how many of these overrepresented categories might apply to you:

- You are a cisgender man.[4]
- You are White.
- You are heterosexual.
- You have no disabilities.
- You speak the majority language in your region.

Can you (and/or your teammates) check most of these boxes? Teams of all overrepresented people have a harder time delivering successful services to vulnerable communities, because the "default" they're likely to build for won't be apt to accommodate the perspectives of marginalized groups. This means a higher risk that the project won't succeed and may even do harm out of ignorance.

---

4 This means that you were both born and identify as a man.

Teams that do user research are hamstrung if they don't have members from all of the relevant language communities able to conduct studies. They can only guess if their products will actually meet the needs of their users. And majority-White teams may not register the impact of historical racism or other discrimination on the foundational rules or practices they seek to strengthen with their product. If the team can even deliver an experience that works for vulnerable users in the first place, they may find that a smoother, "more intuitive" digital interface ends up further entrenching the unfairness.

Government, especially local government, is substantially better at reflecting the local public than the tech industry is. Simply because of the demographics of public service,[5] a career government staffer is also far more likely than a technologist to be a woman and/or a person of color. Yet even government agencies tend to become whiter and more monolingual at more senior levels. Local governments in my home state of California, for example, hire tons of frontline staff who are bilingual in Spanish or Chinese, but conduct almost all administrative-level government work in English.

Privilege can also exist in power dynamics between the makers of a product and its users, especially if it's something people are required to use in a difficult situation.

Designing interfaces that only work for people with access to a computer is a perfect example. While the vast majority of Americans have some access to the internet in 2020, a large minority use a phone as their primary access point,[6] and may not ever use a computer. When American school districts shifted suddenly to online classes during the 2020 pandemic, many students who access the internet on their phones,

---

5 Government service is much more diverse than the tech industry. See for example Todd Gardner, "The Racial and Ethnic Composition of Local Government Employees in Large Metro Areas: 1960-2010," Center for Economic Studies, US Census Bureau, August 2013, https://www2.census.gov/ces/wp/2013/CES-WP-13-38.pdf.

6 According to the Pew Internet and American Life project, as of 2019, 37 percent of Americans access the internet primarily through a mobile device. See Monica Anderson, "Mobile Technology and Home Broadband 2019," Pew Research Center, Internet & Tech, June 13, 2019, https://www.pewresearch.org/internet/2019/06/13/mobile-technology-and-home-broadband-2019/.

or whose families didn't have a separate computer for every person in school, were left out.

Not accounting for the potential for abuse and harassment is another frequent example. This might seem like an edge case to anyone who's from a group that doesn't experience daily harassment, but if the team includes women, LGBT people, and people of color who feel empowered to share their perspectives, they will likely make this a priority.

None of this means you can't do effective work in civic tech as someone from an overrepresented category. It just means you need to regularly check your privilege—and check in with less privileged people—in order to do so.

MAKING CIVIC TECH FOR EVERYONE

For many services, government can be thought of as a monopoly provider that has both a legal and a moral responsibility to serve everyone. If a courthouse is not ADA accessible, a person with a mobility challenge can't take their case to a competing legal provider down the street that will welcome their power chair. If your town's website uses a low color-contrast ratio, or fails to caption images, it will be that much harder for people with visual challenges to access information and use online services.

Many practitioners still dismiss these considerations as "edge cases," which shows a real lack not just of empathy, but of imagination. Technology offers useful capabilities to people with all kinds of mobility, perception, and cognitive challenges; it just has to be planned and tested in order to work. People in civic tech can see this as an opportunity to push back on assumptions about the way technology is built. There are online products[7] to help you assess basics like reading level, acceptable contrast for colorblind users, and whether screen readers can parse the image captions in your content management system (CMS). There's no excuse not to avail yourself of these tools if you're building software.

---

7 accessibility.digital.gov keeps an up to date set of resources.

One of the most interesting aspects of technology in the civic context is the hard constraint that the product you build must serve *everyone*. It's true that current prototyping and rapid development tools are poorly suited to build interfaces for a multilingual, multi-ability society. But that's a *technology* problem—if anyone can figure it out, it's probably us.

There's an encouraging template in the US Web Design System[8] that, in just a few years, went from an experiment with basic accessibility to a pattern library with multiple accessible color palettes, type profiles, and complex web components. Maybe you're on the team that can create the multilingual-by-default, reading-level-checking, accessibility-baked-in prototyping suite that would give every civic project in the nation a boost in the right direction.

BEING AN ALLY

In general, the best thing to do if you have substantial privilege is to use it to support underrepresented colleagues and partners. You can do this in many ways:

- Take extra care to make sure that underrepresented colleagues get credit for their ideas and their work.
- Check every idea you come up with and see if it is really new; if it's not, insist on credit for the person or people who came up with it.
- Make sure underrepresented people don't end up doing menial tasks (like note-taking at meetings) more often than others.
- Resolve to limit your speaking time in meetings and respectfully ask for more comments from people who may be overlooked.

• • •

It's important to become aware of your own privileges so you can understand how they affect your relationships with your users,

---

8 designsystem.digital.gov, in v2.7 as of summer 2020.

teammates, and stakeholders. If you're a person with substantial privilege, people may feel less confident speaking freely to you. This is because of the power those privileges carry, which can and has been used to hurt people. It's on you to make it clear that you're aware of it, open to feedback, and intending to use your privilege for good.

Make sure you balance working situations by insisting that the perspectives of those without the same privilege be included and considered. Think hard about what you need to do to gain trust with members of underrepresented communities, including people you want to build good software for. Without addressing your privilege, it's impossible to create truly inclusive products or teams, both of which should be goals for civic tech.

CHAPTER 3
WAYS TO CONTRIBUTE

The opportunity to make an impact for good is the main reason people feel called to civic tech projects, even choosing them over better-paid private-sector tech. In my experience, there's so much useful work that needs to be done that it can be hard to choose what to do.

Where you begin will depend on your values as well as your capabilities. Do you want to strengthen a status quo you believe to be good, or are you more intent on shifting something fundamental in an institution or in society at large? Different approaches and partnership styles, as well as specific missions, will better serve these different goals. Exploring your motivations more deeply can help you decide whom to work with.

As you think broadly about your motivations, these questions may help guide you toward specific mission areas:

- What do you think of as "good" in society?
- What is currently in the way of that good happening?
- What change do you want to see in the world as
  a result of your and others' civic work?

There are multiple ways to get involved; many types of project goals, topical domains, and levels of government and NGO institutions can use the help of civic technologists. In this chapter, I'll discuss the most successful models for sustained work that have emerged in the past decade. Each of the models I'll present has transactional aspects, but I want to emphasize that all of them are political. Not partisan, but necessarily political.

Trying to effect change in the relationship between the public and the government, regardless of means you use, is an act of politics. The methods you use and the partnerships you enter either reinforce or change existing power dynamics—and their beneficiaries. Power-shifting may or may not be among your motivations for entering civic tech, but it will always be a potential consequence of your work.

STEPPING FORWARD: VOLUNTEER COLLABORATIONS

Joining a volunteer civic group is probably the best way to start doing civic tech part-time. There are no entry requirements; civic groups are specifically set up to onboard newcomers, and usually all that is required is registering for a meeting. Depending on their capacity, funding structure, and length of service, the groups may have all kinds of onboarding materials, shovel-ready projects, and mentors available to new members. They don't require a specific commitment of time, and are very flexible and open to project proposals—but of course as pro bono volunteer work, this work is unpaid (except for a few leadership positions in well-funded groups).

The civic tech movement in the United States began on the municipal level with a few small internal groups and thousands of volunteers. Cities were quick to embrace the idea of community hackathons and the open-data movement in the early 2010s, and this led to the establishment of regular tech volunteer meetings in many large and medium-sized cities. Code for Tulsa, for example, has been meeting weekly since 2011, even running remotely during 2020's COVID-19 quarantine. Many of these groups formalized through Code for America's Brigade program or became independent nonprofit organizations.

These groups partner directly with local government agencies. In many cities, the Chief Data Officer (if the city has one) is a regular attendee, and department staff who want to engage the group's help will bring their challenges (and their data) to meetings. Related community organizations often bring their knowledge and understanding of challenges as well. Members self-organize and commit to working on specific aspects of development or design challenges. Members can also propose work to local agencies.

Many volunteer groups have a particularly strong practice in opening data; they depend on it for their project work, and they're often culturally aligned with both the open-source and open-data movements.[1] You're likely to meet people who feel passionate about all types of open data, especially maps—cities and states have enormous amounts of interesting geodata. Advocacy for more data, more transparency, and more partnership at the municipal level has made a huge contribution to the strength of civic tech in the United States.

Over the long term, things that start out as prototypes created by these trusted groups of volunteers are often adopted and brought into a city's internal tech stack. Once a service becomes important to a government's operations, they want to pay for it to ensure that they'll be able to get support. Therefore, a city might ask a group to spin up a start-up in order to sell the software to them. Standout volunteers have also been hired directly by cities to continue and expand the work they do, and dedicated volunteer groups have several times convinced cities to establish data positions or internal digital groups.

---

1 There's a strong thread in civic tech from the open-source movement and a closely allied government-transparency movement. The Sunlight Foundation was one of the first institutional players in US civic tech, and its focus has always been transparency.

THE BUSINESS OF GOVERNMENT TECH: STARTUPS AND OTHER VENDORS

There is an entire ecosystem of companies that have government as their intended primary customer. Some of these companies are set up to serve specific government use cases (recording public meetings and making the recordings available online, for example), while others offer goods or services that are optimized for government purchasing and processes.

Much of the start-up ecosystem in this field is focused on city and county governments. This is a substantial market, as there are about three thousand counties and some twenty thousand cities and towns in the United States. Many cities and counties have procurement authorities that allow them to engage with (relatively) small companies for (relatively) small engagements, via request for proposal (RFP) processes that are relatively informal. You don't necessarily need an entire department to win government business at these levels, but you do need someone in your company to become expert at it, and you need to be able to work with a slower sales cycle

Playing at the federal and state level, compared to the municipal level, calls for more specific focus on positioning your business within the community of government vendors (known as "industry" in the federal tech community). If you become certified as a Small Business Administration 8(a) Small Business, a Woman-Owned Small Business (WOSB), or a Service-Disabled Veteran-Owned Small Business (SDVOSB), just to name a few, there are many opportunities to compete for federal and state business.

If you want to start a company focused on governments or institutional NGOs, you will need to design your product-development processes around an institutional sales cycle, and you'll need to vet funders carefully to make sure they understand the differences in runway and growth curve. If you want to work for such a company, you'll need an understanding of government needs and an alignment with the mission, but the hiring process will be much like a typical private-sector process.

GOING ALL IN: INNOVATION LABS
AND DIGITAL SERVICE TEAMS

In the past ten years, the United States federal government and many large city governments have established internal digital groups directed by the executive. State governments, somewhat later, are doing the same. These come in two types—innovation labs and digital service teams—but they are often a first and second stage of the same initiative, so it's worth talking about them together.

Innovation labs are set up to bring ideas and talent from the private sector into special spaces in government that have a higher risk tolerance than usual.[2] They correspond closely to the "showing what's possible" demonstration strain of civic tech, often focusing on opening data, prototyping, and working with members of the public and volunteers to test new ideas. They're small, nimble, and (if successful) often succeeded by a digital service group.

Digital service groups distinguish themselves from innovation labs in that their mission is typically building production-grade software and service designs rather than prototypes (the "doing what's necessary" side). Their work may include migrating legacy systems to new tech stacks, as well as introducing new design methods. Most model themselves after the UK's Government Digital Service, a high-level team with executive sponsorship, working with significant organizational power on executive priorities.

The term "digital service" or "digital team" is common for these groups. They also often refer to the work they do as "building digital services" (another GDS-ism), so the language can be a bit confusing. In contrast

---

2 Innovation labs have a lot of history. Programs like the Mayor's Office of New Urban Mechanics in Boston and Philadelphia, and the Mayor's Office of Civic Innovation in San Francisco, led the charge for civic technology inside of government. The federal Office of Personnel Management had an early innovation lab in the 2010s as well, and Todd Park, then US CTO, had his advisors working on an "entrepreneur in residence" idea that led to the Presidential Innovation Fellows program. At the same time as these were being founded, the federal General Services Administration (GSA) was running its Office of Citizen Service and Innovative Technology.

to an innovation lab or a volunteer group, a digital service group typically requires employees to work on projects that have been chosen by the executive and funded by the legislature in advance. The missions are broad, and the cultures open, but the specific project work may offer little opportunity for pet initiatives; the model for these teams is truly service, and members are expected to follow directives.

WHAT ABOUT 18F?

One of the best-known digital teams in the United States also happens to be one of the more accessible ways to join federal civic technology: 18F, an organization within the General Service Administration.[3] Its activities are similar to the United States Digital Service (USDS), which reports to the White House chain of command, but its structure is different. Like almost every other GSA office, it operates without its own congressional budget appropriation and gets its funding from customers.

Most of these customers are federal agencies, along with a few state agencies. And because it's operating as a paid service, 18F priorities are those of government customers rather than the White House (though the White House is occasionally a customer as well). If you join USDS or one of the state-level digital services, you can guess based on administration priorities what you might be working on, but 18F works on needs agencies themselves identify and collaborates intentionally with agencies that want to advance their digital practices.

Thanks to GSA's forward-thinking policies on remote work, 18F is a distributed organization that people can join from anywhere. Its application process is similar to that of innovation labs and digital service teams, but the whole thing is likely to be conducted remotely.

---

3 The curious name refers to the location of the main GSA building (18th and F Street in Washington, DC).

FOR THE PEOPLE, BY THE PEOPLE: CITIZEN ENGAGEMENT AND MUTUAL AID

You don't actually have to partner directly with government to be part of civic tech. There are any number of worthwhile efforts that focus on bringing communities together and holding their governments accountable. *Citizen engagement* projects give constituents channels to understand and express opinions about public debates, while *mutual aid* projects help individuals help each other without government or institutional participation. Many of the NGOs in both of these spaces need help from technologists.

Most developed examples of this category are incorporated as nonprofits, either 501(c)3 charitable organizations or 501(c)4 educational organizations. This allows them to accept foundation funding (and individual donations for a 501(c)3). Some operate entirely on membership contributions and volunteer labor.

One interesting example is Recovers.org, a nonprofit that helps communities communicate and share resources after natural disasters. Founded as a civic start-up in 2012, it later incorporated as a separately named, formal 501(c)3 that accepts donations. It lets people set up specialized websites with the formula [city].recovers.org, and has been used by both community groups and government agencies. This isn't something that is likely to attract VC money, nor would it be easy for a local community to build well in a time of need. It's not something the federal government has a program to provide to states or cities, either— it's a true mutual-aid model.

Streetmix.net, a citizen engagement app that lets people design streetscapes for collaborative planning processes, ran as a volunteer project for several years. It began at a Code for America hackathon, and the creators eventually obtained foundation sponsorship that sustains it as an open-source project and keeps it free to use. To date, it has been used to create more than a hundred thousand plans, but it has never had paid staff or direct revenue.

Financial sustainability over time is the biggest challenge for projects like this, as they don't generate direct revenue and both foundation grants and individual donations take time and persistence to pursue. These skills are less common in technology founding teams, but if you have them, starting something like this is a path worth considering.

These projects have in common that they aim directly at a specific civic good, without necessarily trying to restructure the practices of an entrenched bureaucracy. As such, they follow different paths to adoption (word of mouth, direct community marketing or advertising). Some focus specifically on a local community, without an ambition to expand. This is a fine model, although the broader civic tech community will welcome stories about successes and permission to imitate.

If you want to start a community project, you'll need community connections. This will be easy if you're already part of the community you hope to serve; if you're not, don't underestimate the work this requires. Do your homework (are you *sure* no one else is already working on this problem?), approach people with humility, and listen deeply.

Also, like any project, these very valuable efforts need a model of sustainability past the prototype stage. I don't say a business model here, because the successful projects in this category are not all organized as traditional businesses. This may on the surface make them seem easier, but that's deceptive—a properly structured charitable non-profit or a robust open-source project that is sustainable over years is at least as challenging from an administrative perspective as a for-profit business.

MAKING PARTNERSHIPS AND SPACES INCLUSIVE

All of the above types of partnership need more Black and brown technologists, and more people with varied language capacities and disabilities. Whatever your own status, but especially if you're a majority person, you can help. As you look for teams to join, or if you decide to start your own initiative, pay attention to the composition of the group and what norms it follows. If your network mostly contains people like you, it's very easy to set up or reinforce exclusionary spaces. It can also be easy to act inappropriately when you go to spaces where other sorts of people are dominant. Act as a guest, and a good guest, if you are invited to spaces for vulnerable people. Demonstrate your respect and offer your skills.

To make sure your group or project is safe and welcoming for underrepresented people (particularly if you yourself are from an overrepresented group), these are some actions you can take:[4]

- Have a diverse founding or leadership team.
- Say publicly (and mean it) that you're actively seeking underrepresented collaborators for key roles.
- Make your online and offline meeting spaces accessible to all.
- Prominently post a code of conduct (especially if this is a hackathon, open-source project, or volunteer meetup) saying that harassment and discrimination won't be tolerated.
- Make sure any code of conduct includes how the group will respond if problems occur.
- Consider anonymous first-round submissions if you're putting on a conference or other event where you ask for proposals.

All of these measures are easier to implement from the beginning of a project or company, but it's never too late. Teams gain both perspective and capacity by being inclusive, and this should be a baseline for any civic technology effort.

• • •

The change you're able to effect will depend on the political factors at play—and all of the models I've discussed here are political to some degree. Working on core mission-critical systems as a volunteer is just very hard to arrange, for example—and creating speculative prototypes as a government employee is equally hard most of the time. Attempts

---

4 There are many references on this that go into far more detail; I share a few in Further Readings.

to transmit good software models from city to city as free open-source offerings have failed multiple times; companies have generally worked better. Getting fully certified as a federal vendor is difficult, but if you want to work on federal problems without joining, it's the right thing to do—so build it into your plan.

You should also consider how ready your potential partners are to work with you.

- Have their leaders shown an interest in modern technology or innovation?
- Have they backed any of that with budget or staff time allocations?
- In conversations with them, how open-minded are they to feedback about their goals and plans, and how ready are they to give direct feedback to you? (Keep in mind: partners who put private-sector tech on a pedestal can be just as hard to collaborate with as those set in their ways.)
- Do they have hiring or contracting authorities ready, through which they can work with you (or your business or group, however it's constituted)?

Some of these, at least, are preconditions for success in any of the above models. It would be ridiculous only to work with partners who are already practicing exactly how you'd hope they would, but it's a recipe for misery to sign on with those who are fully committed to practices you think are antithetical to the change you aspire to drive. Finding or creating the right situation to do the work you want isn't always easy, but having a template for engaging should help.

CHAPTER 4

PROJECT TYPES

The technical needs of many government agencies and civic groups are relatively simple: good websites, good databases, and good APIs, everywhere, go a long way toward enabling more responsive constituent-government relationships. But contemplating a roadmap to "everywhere" is daunting, and of course what makes a website or API "good" varies depending on what you're trying to accomplish and who the users are.

Once you've identified an area that excites you, consider a few specifics about how your involvement might work. In thinking about how to personally get involved with projects, I find this list of questions helpful:

- Where would I act in order to relieve the most pain for users?
- Where would I act in order to relieve pain and free up capacity for maintainers/stewards?
- Where would I act to make sure my changes last?
- Where can I get access and support to act?

If you're starting a project, it's really useful to be able to review ongoing or past similar projects to understand the challenges. Projects aimed at similar goals can even offer lessons in how to shape your own effort. And while you may not have completely free choice of projects if you join a government digital service team, it will still be helpful to be able to identify the common types when you're assigned to one. The following sections outline a few categories of civic technology projects that can address common challenges faced by governments and civic organizations.

SERVICE DELIVERY PROJECTS

Many of the best-known civic tech projects are in the area of *service delivery*, which means performing the public services that a government institution is required (and funded) to provide. This broad category includes a little bit of everything, from public benefits enrollment to recreation programming on the local level, all the way up to registering to vote, getting a passport, and paying income taxes on the state and federal levels. Basically, service delivery projects do what a private-sector company might think of as customer interaction—serving the meals for a restaurant, or selling people tickets and flying the planes for an airline.

Service delivery is attractive for technology solutions because the private sector has become very adept at delivering services of various kinds online. These are also projects that can have a direct, visible impact on members of the public. (Though that impact can cut both ways if something is done poorly or incompletely!)

Working on service delivery almost always requires direct support from a government entity or an agency with a robust open-data practice. Quite a few government datasets and APIs are openly available, allowing companies or volunteer groups to create alternate front-ends to official services.[1]

---

1 The easiest way to find open data is to look for data.[city or state].gov, or just data.gov for the federal government.

Service delivery improvement goals are most often pursued in place with a specific agency or locality, or as product strategies by independent companies. When considering how to approach a service delivery project, you need to understand the underlying need, the existing systems, and the business processes in place to deliver the service now. Look out for players, either individual or organizational, who benefit from the current status quo, and consider how you'll overcome their preferences. Knowing about existing legal or regulatory restrictions is almost always useful as well.

Just like in the private sector, civic service delivery interfaces live and die by adoption. It has to be better than the current interface to succeed—and further, it has a responsibility not to leave people behind. That's a worthy standard for any online service, and not easy to meet because of the breadth of the public and the nature of our actual needs. The more representative your team is of the population it aims to serve, the better equipped you'll be to develop a successful interface.

INFRASTRUCTURE AND DATA PROJECTS

Many of the excellent services available to paying customers in the private sector are underpinned by significant investments in infrastructure like cloud hosting, web content management systems, analytics suites, and credit-card processing platforms. (Think of all the small and medium businesses that use Square or Shopify to accept payments.) Some of these services are available to governments, but they may be much harder to access. Upgrading government and civic infrastructure to allow greater nimbleness and lower costs is another worthwhile type of project.

Upgrades to civic digital infrastructure come in several flavors. Even clearing barriers to adopting best-in-class infrastructure products can be a huge and valuable lift (and is accessible for non-engineer civic tech practitioners). You might:

- research where government procurement rules intersect with private-sector pricing models and payment practices, and help align them;
- educate interested government officials on how to ask their IT departments for better systems; or
- set up special purchasing authorities.[2]

You generally have to join a government to work directly on deep infrastructure, but even if you aren't empowered to touch the code yourself, you may be able to help by performing technical assessments that officials can use to seek budget support or force accommodations (for example, API upgrades) from vendors. Questions like "When does it make sense to update versus migrate a system?" and "What might be gained (and lost) by moving to a cloud-based architecture?" require both strong technical understanding and the ability to articulate trade-offs to non-technical management and contracting specialists.

One of the strongest infrastructure plays we can make as civic technologists is to work on data projects. There are few useful services that don't depend on data, and having it available in a convenient, machine-readable format is a precondition for all kinds of further building and action.[3] In many places within the public sector, valuable data is on paper in binders and file cabinets; many digital systems are merely containers for scanned, unindexed PDFs. Getting information from any of those files involves having a human read them.

Managing machine-readable data requires an entirely different class of infrastructure. Working on these issues can be extremely powerful, and requires a high level of trust with public-sector partners charged with stewardship of public information. There are some avenues to do it from outside government, but if you are really excited to work with this level of

2 18F and the Federal Acquisitions Service did this in 2015 with their Agile Blanket Purchase Agreement. The Agile BPA allowed vendors to demonstrate Agile capabilities by creating prototypes and then joining a pool of verified, federally approved companies to provide those new-to-government services.

3 I intentionally didn't say *open* data, because having the data in the first place is a precondition for opening it up for public review and use.

depth, figuring out how to join the government agency you want to work with is probably your best option.

Safely opening data for outside public use is one more step that practitioners can advocate for and help with. If records kept by government agencies are computerized, they become data usable by computer applications, when and if practitioners can get access. This requires work to review, clean, standardize, post, and maintain datasets.

At the local levels, there is more openness to collaboration with volunteers and nonprofit groups for these projects. This is partly because of the recent history of city-based open-data and civic hacking groups, and partly because cities have fewer rules constraining working with such groups (and lower budget resources in general). Volunteer partnerships have had great success safely opening data for outside public use in the past decade, with civic tech practitioners acting as both open-data advocates and advisors to mayors and other officials across the United States.

Data-driven projects can easily expand into the areas of civic engagement and mutual aid. Covidtracking.com, organized in the spring of 2020 by two reporters from the *Atlantic* and a small army of volunteers, became the primary source for aggregated data on coronavirus cases and tests in the United States. It's a massive effort that collates new statistics from state health departments daily, and publishes charts and downloadable raw data online.

Community projects like this may also make use of public data to offer citizens information on how their elected representatives vote and how to contact them,[4] or—in a less automated way—connect people in debt to a public utility with people who can donate money to pay off those debts.[5]

---

4 POPVOX and GovTrack.us are two examples with different purposes.
5 The Human Utility is just one example of this kind of project (https://detroitwaterproject.org/).

SPECIALIZED TOOLS FOR DIGITAL GOVERNMENT

If you go to your city's website, you'll probably find a prominent link to pay a parking ticket. Click on that link and you'll find yourself whisked off to a payment portal, almost certainly created by one of two companies. It is probably not well designed, and may not be as robust as it could be. This is just one example of the kinds of tools governments need.

Some tools commonly found in the private sector are nevertheless most valuable when they are set up specifically for government use. When I was part of a team that aimed to build a specialized CMS for municipal government websites, we discovered during our research stage that websites for cities and towns present a very different use case from most private-sector websites. Rather than a collection of media or a sales funnel, municipal websites need to point users to two hundred to three hundred task flows that, for any given user, are rarely engaged.

Private-sector web products, from content management systems to analytics suites, embed assumptions about what types of websites they will be used to build, or else require really substantial customization to implement. While many large cities now have strong digital teams that have custom-built what they need, there's still a market for a product like that for smaller governments—if someone can do it at the right price point with the right features.

The US Web Design System (USWDS) is one effort that has endeavored to fill this need. Initially launched as an experiment by Mollie Ruskin of the US Digital Service and Maya Ben-Ari of 18F in 2015, it is now a full-featured, accessibility-checked, free design system supported as part of the General Service Administration's Digital.gov. Numerous federal and state agencies use it as a basis for mobile-responsive, accessible websites to serve constituents in all kinds of ways.

However, most tooling projects begin outside of government as a product, which makes this a very interesting area to look into if you want to start a company. There's a whole ecosystem of for-profit companies, from major enterprises (Xerox, for example, is one of the parking ticket payment companies) to start-ups, working to make things easier for the agencies that provide the services.

Companies that specialize in this area need to fully understand government purchasing and adoption cycles (even if the end product is free). They'll often do multilayered user research with the officials who run the program their products target, as well as the end users of *those* programs. Customer support may also come into play, especially for projects in one of the areas government officials sometimes call "dial-tone services"—meaning anything the public would expect to be always available.

SWOOPING IN FOR A RESCUE

One special category of civic tech engagement is the rescue project. This is a sudden, intense engagement to rapidly scale up (or sometimes repair) some form of tech capacity for a government agency.

A classic example of this comes from 2013, when dozens of tech employees were urgently summoned to Washington to restore the HealthCare.gov website, which crashed catastrophically at launch and threatened to sink one of the top policy priorities of the Obama admin-istration.[6] And as I draft this chapter in the spring of 2020, technologists are mobilizing to help governments deal with the consequences of the COVID-19 pandemic and the quarantine, building eligibility interfaces for loans and unemployment and helping governments scale up. Like political campaigns, these efforts have limited time frames, but can be all-consuming while they're ongoing.

If you're already comfortable with institutional messes, and your personal situation allows you to commit major time to a sudden engagement, these can be enormous service opportunities.[7] But I don't

---

6 Robinson Meyer detailed the story of this rescue in a compelling article. See Meyer, "The Secret Startup That Saved the Worst Website in America, " *Atlantic*, July 9, 2015, https://www.theatlantic.com/technology/archive/2015/07/the-secret-startup-saved-healthcare-gov-the-worst-website-in-america/397784/.

7 It's worth noting that rescue efforts are often done on a volunteer basis (at least in the beginning).

recommend them as a first foray into civic tech; both the intensity and criticality of rescue efforts make them a poor fit for technologists who are also dealing with the steep learning curve of how things work in government. While almost everyone in the HealthCare.gov rescue was new to government tech in 2013, there's now a consensus that anyone doing this should have proven skills and know (as much as possible) what they're getting into.

FORMS: THE BIGGEST BANG FOR THE LEAST TECH

I would be remiss if I didn't talk about forms as a major area of needed work in citizen-government interaction. An enormous number of interactions with government, certainly with executive-branch agencies or courts, involve filling out a form—and most of these forms are confusing, hard to read, and repetitive.

Granted, it's not the cutting edge of software innovation—but improving forms, either by better designing paper ones or creating great, accessible, mobile-capable web ones, can be a significant boost to people's direct experience with government. Individual cities[8] and companies like SeamlessDocs or CityGrows have taken on a number of interesting initiatives in the past few years to help automate forms and their processing at larger scale. But the problem is absolutely vast and will require a variety of solutions.

You can easily contribute your labor to this cause if you're coming from the design or information architecture disciplines.[9]

---

8 Josh Gee's account of doing this work for the city of Boston is worth a read. See Gee, "What I Learned in Two Years of Moving Government Forms Online," Medium, February 22, 2018. https://medium.com/@jgee/what-i-learned-in-two-years-of-moving-government-forms-online-1edc4c2aa089.

9 In the early years of the Consumer Financial Protection Bureau (CFPB), one of the team's major wins was redesigning the required disclosure forms for home mortgages to be more readable and to highlight critical information for borrowers. See the CFPB Mortgage Disclosure Team, "Know before You Owe: Preparing to Finalize the New Mortgage Disclosure Forms," CFPB, November 22, 2013, https://www.consumerfinance.gov/about-us/blog/know-before-you-owe-preparing-to-finalize-the-new-mortgage-disclosure-forms/.

Especially if you are willing and able to help public servants use tools like Microsoft Word or an older CMS to design more usable forms, you can do this kind of work on a relatively short time line (although regulatory or political approval will likely take some time). One of the best things about this is that most forms are public whether on paper or on the web; if you help an agency put forward a good design, it can be easily copied all over the country.

There are strategies for forms in the tools and infrastructure categories too. Rather than redesigning individual forms, you might have the opportunity to create libraries of well-designed form elements (or repurpose existing ones for government use cases), or to work on the data infrastructure required to allow web forms to write directly to databases and skip a reentry step (yes, reentry of data is very common as of now). At many levels, poor form design blocks efficient administration and public confidence in institutions, and any progress, especially when publicly shared, helps the entire field.

• • •

The important thing about discovering where you can use your abilities to greatest effect is to understand what kind of work you're taking on, what kind of partnership and time are required to achieve your goals, and what kind of skills you need to succeed. Depending on where you are and what your goal is, you may be looking at a long time frame; thinking about how to pace yourself and structure the work sustainably will be important.

As you try to determine where to start, think about areas of particular interest and explore efforts already underway in your local or professional community. Many advocates and NGOs can also use help from technologists in categories similar to the ones mentioned above, and they may already have strong relationships with any government partners who need to be involved. Issue campaigns, too, may welcome help. In short, whatever your skill set, there is high-impact work you can do to improve the use of technology in the civic sphere.

CHAPTER 5

INNOVATION AND ITS DISCONTENTS

When it comes to funding, generating early-stage enthusiasm, and connecting with partners, innovation is a good thing. "Government innovation" and "civic innovation" are sometimes even used interchangeably with "civic tech". But at this point in the field's adolescence, most veteran civic technologists can't stand the word.

The main reason for this is because there is a huge gap between what is at the cutting edge in the technology industry right now and the methods and materials that are most useful for government—and *that* can be a challenge to navigate.

Some of the best technologies for government are anything but innovative. Good old databases are typically much more deployable than blockchain technology. The mobile web continues to outperform native apps as a way to offer digital services to everyone, even people who primarily access the internet on their phone. Cloud hosting and services are making inroads, but there are legitimate worries about how to duplicate the security of isolated data centers for certain purposes. AI and machine learning for government use cases are highly controversial because of concerns about privacy and bias.

In this chapter, I'll unpack the idea of innovation and look at where it does and doesn't help us do the right thing. I'll also discuss alternative ways of framing change to institutions and assessing whether newer methods are suitable.

INNOVATION IS A FLAWED FRAMEWORK FOR CHANGE

Our particular wave of civic tech likes to compare itself, somewhat unfairly, to the standard of a particular kind of technology start-up—well-funded, with access to plenty of solid hires and as much of the latest tooling as it wants. Compared to the private-sector tech industry, government is underresourced, less nimble, and far more risk-averse. But when civic and government leadership aspire to private-sector agility, it can be easy to think that the difference lies in innovation and new ideas.

Government work does tend to be slower and less adaptive (and we'll get into regulation in the next chapter). Sometimes innovation provides a necessary shield to allow experimentation with modern risk-amelioration processes like user research and prototyping. Efforts designated as "innovation" may also be able to use relaxed or special hiring practices to bring in people with skills that are missing in the core staff of an agency. The most useful thing about innovation within government is that using it can make it possible to break out separate streams of work that are allowed to take a higher risk profile than an agency typically supports[1].

It's also not uncommon that funding for innovation projects is easier to get than, say, for reform and improvement projects (even if the difference is mainly in the name). Explicit innovation projects have a relatively short track record, so there aren't a hundred years of mixed results to pick apart

---

1 Projects within the innovation stream may or may not actually be high-risk, but they would be regarded as such if the agency has commonly managed risk through comprehensive requirements-gathering and waterfall development. And just because technologists wouldn't consider a project inherently high-risk, that doesn't mean it doesn't pose real risk to a career staffer's status.

in evaluating whether a new one is a good idea. For a lot of tech-enamored administrators, it seems like the simplest way forward: think outside the box and *innovate*, like they do at tech companies.

But there's a falseness to setting innovation as a goal. Newness does not closely correspond to fitness for purpose, and the latter is far more important in mission organizations. Newness in a technical sense may place a government or civic interface out of reach of many of the participants it is required to serve. The assumption that everything requires brand-new thought leads to ignoring many opportunities. Further, if our networks and knowledge of history are weak (and that applies to very many of us in civic tech at present), we may be completely mistaken about whether an idea is *actually* new.

We also lose out when we subscribe to the idea that innovation has to come from outside government (which is implied by setting up special teams to bring in outside people to do it). This attitude overlooks the innovative work that career staff are already doing. Innovation as a concept would seem to favor completely new ideas and revolutionary leaps, but consider just how much of the programming keeping the world running still happens in Excel.[2] It requires a whole lot of creativity to adapt a tool to this degree—and I don't know a much better definition of the useful kind of innovation than that. One of the best things you can do is find people who have created innovative workarounds and hacks in any arena, using the tools they have, and do what you can to empower them. If you're going to accept innovation as a description of your own work, make sure that light shines on them as well.

The most important goal for civic programs is not that they are newer but that they are better. To succeed, we need a nuanced understanding of where newer methods and platforms actually drive better results, which means a clear strategic understanding of "better" for a particular context. And yet, relatively speaking, if in 2020 we're advancing methods

---

2 Martin Fowler, "Illustrative Programming," martinfowler.com, June 30, 2009, https://martinfowler.com/bliki/IllustrativeProgramming.html.

and practices to the 2010s from the 1990s and helping make things better for the public, that *is* a kind of judicious innovation.

BUREAUCRACY AND STEWARDSHIP

The civil service that performs most of the actual work of delivering government to the public is designed to be a long-term institution. Its role is very specifically to provide continuity across the partisan shifts and fads of mere administrations, which come and go. This can be frustrating to changemakers, but as the saying goes, it's a feature, not a bug. If it throws friction in the way of an administration you agree with rapidly implementing policies you like, it also throws friction in the way of an administration you disagree with rapidly implementing policies you don't like.

In its best guise, bureaucracy—the mountains of knowledge work performed every day to keep programs, agencies, and offices actively and accountably serving the public as they should—comes from an ethic of stewardship. Stewardship isn't something the private-sector tech industry talks about very much. (I wish it did more.) But in government, stewardship is a central value. When a government service is supposed to be available for all, it matters very much that there are checks to make sure it really is equitable in its delivery and processes. Websites and software applications are in the class of services that must be available for all, and in particular that must meet the requirements of the Americans with Disabilities Act[3] and related laws—they are public accommodations.

Being public means something important, and the people who process all the forms are doing an important part of being public. Are they always doing it in a perfect way? Of course not. Are there many instances where processes intended to better steward public funds or resources end up doing the exact opposite because they're poorly designed or implemented? So many. It's worth improving both of these things. But if

---

3 Specifics of these requirements are spelled out in the ADA Tool Kit (https://www.ada.gov/pcatoolkit/chap5toolkit.htm).

you don't understand them from a perspective of stewardship in the first place, you won't be able to improve them successfully.

Of course there are a few bad actors in the system, from individuals using interpretations of the rules to build fiefdoms and silos to profiteering companies gatekeeping various kinds of contracts. But the practice of considering change carefully and not moving fast and breaking things on the public dime is a sound practice at heart. Making it safe to move a little faster and fix things—with deliberation and with the public interest always in mind—doesn't have quite the same ring, but it respects the central value of the public service environment.

One thing we sometimes forget is that private-sector time lines are not as fast as they might seem. Amazon Prime launched in 2005, eleven years after Earth's Biggest Bookstore. Google was a search engine with a successful ad business until Gmail launched in 2004. Prime and Gmail are part of the background now, but it took a while for them to become that. To use an even older example, people have been talking about the paperless office since the 1970s, and seriously suggesting it would come about soon since Pagemaker and Quark Xpress launched (following personal computers) in the late '80s. But it really didn't exist anywhere until around 2010 or 2012—and even in 2020, it's only forward-thinking tech or creative offices where the sight of a printout is rare.

It's fair to note, too, that most start-ups that fit the stereotype aren't active in life-critical areas. If you look at technology groups in regulated industries like finance or medicine, or institutional areas like legal tech, you will find challenges and time lines that more resemble what we see in government. Even Google has a famously elaborate planning process known as *objectives and key results* (OKRs)[4] that takes weeks of the company's time. Google has the technical capacity to do things fast, but it and its fellow large technology companies like Facebook and Apple are now grappling with their responsibilities not to break important points of public reliance.

---

4 Google's Objectives and Key Results-based planning process is famous, but their public playbook (https://www.whatmatters.com/resources/google-okr-playbook/) doesn't cover the rounds of negotiation necessary to reconcile goals across departments and divisions.

PERSPECTIVES ON RISK AND FAILURE

In well-resourced tech organizations, it's accepted that we should embrace risk and celebrate failure, because it's all learning, which is always good. It's true that nothing new can be made without some risk, but technologists are often too cavalier about failure even in their own arena. We've seen company collapses that put thousands of people out of work celebrated by founders for new insights that they gained—at the expense of millions of dollars of investors' money[5].

Failure takes a different cast when the money involved is precious taxpayer dollars and the services provided are life-critical—as does risk, when there's more separation between organizational risk and personal risk. There's a stronger drive to somehow fix or hang on to efforts that are showing problems, rather than throw away the resources already spent. The government press can also be brutal in covering early failures that the tech press would often chalk up to learning. Hanging on isn't always the right decision, and in fact it's sometimes called the sunk-cost fallacy, but it's understandable if you know how much harder those resources are to come by, and how high the reputational risk of being seen to waste public funds is.[6]

So, given that innovation requires some level of risk-taking, and certain risks are very dangerous in a government context, how do you proceed? Technologists' best option is often to start with something very small— ideally so small that several iterations can be completed in a span of months. For example, iterative software development, done well in any of its various flavors, demonstrably results in better outcomes than large procurements specified entirely up front.

There's an entire architecture of regulation and culture that supports the kind of risk-management that comes from specifying hundreds of

---

5 So many postmortems of WeWork illustrate this, but some examples are more delectable than others. See Noah Kulwin, "The Extremely Bad Vibes of Adam Neumann," *Outline*, September 19, 2019, (https://theoutline.com/post/7982/adam-neumann-wework-absurd).

6 Even medium-high government officials have to take out professional liability insurance policies because they could be personally named in a lawsuit against their agency.

pages of requirements and having everybody follow the direction of their superiors to the letter. That makes it hard to "just start iterating" on anything substantial—but doing something like building an application form that gets great reviews, in a matter of months, can open the conversation. Getting permission to try something as challenging as a new approach to risk management, which will take years, requires showing it at the microscale of a few months first.

THE ROLE OF PROTOTYPES

Nearly every civic technology project begins with a prototype. This has pluses and minuses. The beauty of prototypes is that they are cheap and ephemeral and can be thrown away; the downside is...that they are cheap and ephemeral and can be thrown away. Prototypes are golden in the "showing what's possible" demonstration stage, but if you want to have a lasting impact, you'll also need a strategy for the operationalization stage that comes afterward.

Nothing beats a working prototype for showing what is possible with modern technology. Prototypes also make it possible to test and uncover user needs at a much higher level of fidelity than abstract discussions about requirements. If you are adept at turning datasets into beautiful, useful web interfaces quickly, you will be a very persuasive advocate for your own methods. A lightweight piece of software is also an incredibly effective argument against a heavyweight requirements process at certain stages, though it doesn't address everything governments may be legitimately concerned with.

The downside of prototypes is that private-sector technologists are trained to use them in a way that assumes an abundance of resources. "We celebrate failure—it's all just learning." "We can just throw it away." Those statements sometimes don't hold true in a lower-resourced, higher-obligation public-sector environment, and not just for reasons of culture. A prototype can be read as a kind of promise—and if you don't have some idea of the path to fulfilling that promise with robust, accessible, production-grade software down the road (what I call the "doing what's necessary" stage, or operationalization), it can be a risky promise.

A working, data-driven prototype offered for live testing to hundreds of agency staffers with an assumption that the team will learn enough to get a second phase funded can degrade during a long budget process, or end up as the only thing that is ever delivered due to an administration change.

Often, in order to move beyond a prototype, a team has to confront the legacy systems in place. Helping move a government agency away from a costly and clunky database architecture (for example) can be one of the biggest possible wins, but it requires long-term focus, significant tech and organizational skill sets, and usually work with procurement and other bureaucratic processes too. As you build any live prototype, it's worth exploring the current system and starting to think about how—in the best case where everyone is excited to make the prototype real—you will grapple with these challenges.

DIGITAL TRANSFORMATION AND CONTINUOUS IMPROVEMENT

It's worth considering how different frames can shape our thinking alongside innovation. One term I haven't mentioned yet is *government digital transformation*, which is often discussed together with civic innovation. We struggled to define it in my time at 18F, although nearly everyone agreed it was an important goal. After a research project addressing the subject, we settled on the idea that a government agency is transformed when it chooses and manages technology effectively in the service of its larger mission, *and* when it's capable of handling the inevitable next technological change on its own.

In other words, an organization has only cleared the hurdle of digital transformation when it's capable of continuous improvement. It's very much worth pointing out that most private-sector organizations haven't cleared this hurdle, either, and many start-ups haven't been through enough changes to know whether their practices are sustainable or not.

Most of the modern practices private-sector technologists prefer assume a continuous, rather than episodic, process of advancing design, technology, and mission fit in concert. This challenges many existing conditions in government, including how technology procurement fits into budgetary cycles, the ability to create staff positions for product managers in addition to developers and designers, and whether delivering digital interfaces is a sideline or a core business.

Continuous improvement is valuable because it suggests that *better* is what matters, and that we have more than one shot at achieving it. It's sometimes described with a metaphor of compound interest; compound improvements build on each other over medium time frames (say ten years), resulting in a situation that is many times better than it was at the start, even if each individual improvement is small.

In my current project, we've adopted a mapping metaphor to keep our expectations for innovation in check. The reasoning goes like this: if we're starting in a situation where we only have paper atlases, we may need to progress through MapQuest before we can get all the way to Google Maps or even Waze. We know that it's technically possible today to deliver real-time traffic with a voice assist, but we also understand the reality of our environment—it's a huge win just to attain on-demand, custom-printable maps from where we started. This kind of relative innovation, put in place alongside the practices that will enable the next leap when it becomes appropriate, can be a very useful frame too.

There are more and less risky areas to work in in the civic space, and it's sometimes possible to create faster change in the less risky ones. This is valuable too; if you make it easier for people to, for example, sign up for summer programs with their city, that's a great thing. If you want to do something (relatively) fast, that kind of work is a great candidate. But if you're working on immigration or criminal justice or disaster aid, it may help to think of yourself as part of a relay. Making these essential functions as good as we, the public, deserve them to be, is going to take a long time.

We're not the first to make progress on this, though, and there are many more eager and capable people where we came from. We need to acknowledge activists and reformers who came before us, from advocates for campaign-finance disclosure to the Clinton-era Re-inventing Government effort (with all their imperfections), and see ourselves as part of a long process.

• • •

Whether the changes civic tech proposes are truly cutting-edge or only new in the government context, framing them in ways that give public-sector partners an easy yes is part of our job—as is backing up that tempting yes by making sure we manage risk well enough not to wreck our partners' careers. So expect to spend more time talking about risk, and more time responding to contingencies, than you would elsewhere. It's worth your time. Innovation is one attractive way to describe what we do, and it resonates with many partners. But we also owe them candid assessments of alternate ways of thinking about change and of when innovation isn't needed. Innovation is a powerful tool, but one to use with care.

CHAPTER 6
WORKING IN REGULATED SPACES

Almost everyone I know who has joined civic tech from the private sector started out with the idea that doing things fast would be part of making things better. It turns out it's possible to go somewhat faster, and it's definitely possible to do better, but there are many reasons why start-up-like time lines aren't practical.

A few things are strikingly different about the public sector, in particular around money. Most private-sector entities are organized around a profit goal and subject to competition, and it's relatively easy to tell whether they are profitable. Government is, of course, funded by taxes on the public, and is generally the only provider of the services it offers. It operates under the principle of stewardship, which means it's not about *making* money, but about taking *responsibility* for it and distributing it wisely.

This adds another dimension to management and to oversight. A government agency is typically supposed to spend its entire budget, and so the question asked by its management isn't whether it took in more than it gave out, but whether it spent the money well: did the public get the expected level of benefit, was that benefit fairly distributed, and was the money spent in a fair manner (no corruption, no discrimination on contracts, etc.)?

Stewardship plays into more careful and risk-averse work styles, and it explains many of the things that tend to puzzle newcomers to the public sphere—including why it seems to take so long to get anything done.

BUDGETS, CYCLES, AND PROCUREMENT

At every level of government, budgets are one of the most contentious and scrutinized types of legislation. Legislatures appropriate most money in one- or two-year cycles, and the specific designated spending requirements have the force of law. You'd think this might mean that you would just need to pick the right starting point, calendar-wise, but it's a little more complicated than that. Negotiations may continue until the last minute (or even after that, in federal budget negotiations[1]). An agency may get much more or much less than expected in budget, which in either direction will require re-configuring their projects.

There are also different "colors" of money, meaning a legislature or funder puts different constraints on how certain money can be spent. Sometimes this has to do with timing: "one-year money" has to be spent during the same budget or grant year, for example, meaning that the agency might have to specially structure a contract to make sure it's completed inside of that timeline, no matter what happens on the project. On the other hand, in most governments, there can be some flexibility around when the money is *obligated*[2] compared to when it is disbursed.

De-obligating money (yes, that is a word) once it has been obligated is an epic bureaucratic pain, so there is a very strong motivation to stick

---

1 The federal government has an option called *continuing resolutions*, where legislators keep negotiating past the deadline—which means old programs can continue, but new programs proposed for the next cycle will have to wait.

2 *Obligating* money (sometimes also called *encumbering*) means contractually committing it to a specific program or vendor for a specific purpose; it is sometimes considered as good as spent once that happens, so there are times when you can obligate your one-year money during the year and actually disburse it during the following year (usually not longer).

with a contract once signed, even if it isn't going well. This is one reason civic technologists should push for smaller contracts with renewal options over huge one-shot contracts; but the epic bureaucratic pain of contracting itself has to be weighed on the other side.

CAPEX AND OPEX

There's one other piece of budget language that you should at least be aware of that crosses private and public sectors. That's CAPEX and OPEX, for *capital expense* and *operating expense,* and they're important because there's often some contention around which one is appropriate for various kinds of technology work— and your best project plan might be very different depending on how you're being funded.

Capital expense, outside of technology budgets, is for something durable like a building or a fleet of trucks. While the money may be used in one year, for budget purposes it will be amortized (counted partially) across the multiple years the asset is in use.

Operating expense is a continuing expense, like salaries, printing, software subscriptions, or utilities. Most legislatures are more worried about increasing operating expenses, since these are seen as increased spending that will continue indefinitely.

Technology projects are often funded as capital expenses, because it can be easier to make the case for one-time outlays. This can be a problem because (as you know if you're a tech person) something like a large website that encompasses, say, 60 percent of an entity's interaction with the public is not something that is ever really finished in the same way a building is. If CAPEX runs out and there's no more money to maintain and sustain the system, the system can deteriorate very quickly.

Both legislative and nonprofit funders tend to look unfavorably on money not getting used up, and legislatures in particular will reduce allocations the next year if an agency returns money from this year. This plays into the interesting possibility of getting extra resources at the end of a budget year, because there's money that needs to be spent (or at least obligated) quickly.

The way governments buy software and technical services, or *procurement*, is strictly regulated for ethical reasons. The rules are intended to discourage profiteering on sales to the government as well as the practice of government officials handing contracts to friends or to companies in which they have a financial interest. However, the rules often do more to confound and complicate than they do to serve these stewardship goals. Requirements that seem to protect the government from contracting with fly-by-night organizations (something like "bidders must have at least twenty employees") will actually exclude many excellent user research firms and not a few development shops, for example.

A very basic procurement process includes:

- an RFI (request for information) where the agency asks for pre-proposals suggesting how much they might pay for a set of services;
- an RFP (request for proposals) with lists of requirements, put together through a long "requirements gathering" process;
- an evaluation process, for which the criteria must be published in advance; depending on the specific rules, quality may or may not be able to be considered, but price always must be;
- awarding the contract to the company with the highest score on the evaluation criteria; and
- actually writing the contract.

Each of these steps has tricky standards and rules, and there are several where your bid can be disqualified for something as simple as a bureaucratic error.[3] The typical process advantages companies that

---

3 I was recently on the evaluation committee for a competitive bid where two candidates were disqualified for not checking all of the boxes on the terms and conditions.

have expertise with government contracting. When the contract is for consulting services in an area the government isn't familiar with (say, UX design or agile development), it gets even harder.

Contracts make deliverables extremely concrete and explicit based on the requirements, and changes to those must be handled formally. If you're a software person, you'll see immediately how this structure, designed for things like pencils or fleets of trucks, is problematic for digital goods. The lowest bidder for a database project is not necessarily the best one for the government to hire. And software projects are notorious for shifting their plans as the team learns in the course of the work. Specifying exact deliverables for even a six-month software project assumes that the team won't learn anything new in the process, and prevents them from changing the plan if they do.

Minor procurements are their own kind of problem. Contracts for much under $25,000 (or more like $100,000 if it's federal) are challenging for many governments, and despite a stated preference for off-the-shelf[4] software, few are able to easily license software-as-a-service (SaaS) products without some amendment to both the license and purchasing process the software companies use with their private-sector customers. In addition to that, each SaaS product will need to be vetted by IT, and depending on the level and function, may need a formal authority to operate (ATO).

REGULATIONS AND TOOLING

As a civic technologist, your best posture is to recognize that the motives behind the regulations are almost always good and important; the regulations themselves are sometimes overinterpreted or misapplied. The implementation of the regulations in process can be truly ripe for reform that will benefit not just self-conscious innovators but many, many public servants trying to do good work. In thinking about where to focus and what to take on, reflect on these questions:

---

4 You might see this as consumer off the shelf (or "COTS") software.

- How dependent is your process on the tooling you prefer? (Would you find it harder if you didn't have access to GitHub? Or Figma? Or Google Docs?)
- How dependent is your project architecture on specific technology components?

Government security requirements apply not only to software built by the government, but to purchased *components* of systems—whether commercial, open-source, or internal. Many of them, depending on the level of government and local specifics, also apply to software used internally for work. At the federal level, getting an ATO[5] is an absolute requirement for anything you build or want to use, and it can be a months-long, formal process in itself to demonstrate that software meets all of the security and accessibility regulations.[6]

Maybe you prefer a particular stack or tool because your team is familiar with it; if so, I hope you'll be flexible enough to work with what's possible when you need to. But it's important to acknowledge how embedded SaaS tooling of various sorts is in both design and engineering processes as of 2020, especially for distributed teams. Many of these tools specifically enable faster or more distributed collaboration, and while it's possible to do it without them, it takes more effort and isn't as fast. This greater friction is another factor in longer time lines and more worn-out teams.

Part of the reason you may find it easier to get access to Microsoft ecosystem products (from Azure to Word) is that Microsoft has prioritized meeting government purchasing requirements. Quite a few software or cloud providers, especially in the SaaS realm, don't or can't.[7] This is one reason federal technologists have been working so hard on cloud.gov, basically a white-label version of AWS that meets all federal security and

---

5 If you're interested, the OpenControl community has solid, simplified content on federal ATOs: https://www.fedramp.gov/issuing-an-authority-to-operate/.

6 A team at 18F has been working for several years on streamlining the ATO process (at least for GSA) and is making headway.

7 One reason for this is that many providers with subscription business models have optimized for credit card payments to the degree that they don't have processes for issuing invoices or accepting other forms of payment. Credit cards are very hard to come by in government, and are often restricted to travel spending if they're available at all.

privacy requirements out of the box and can be paid for with interagency agreements to the General Services Administration. The existence of such a platform will lop months off of many federal technology projects, and there are plans to make it available to state and local government customers too.

Finally, you can expect the formality, and therefore the friction, of all reviews to be higher and for each step to take a bit longer. There are places where this could be reduced, and it's a great side effort for your team to do so. That said, reform is difficult organizational work (and in fact will slow you down further even if it speeds future efforts), and you may decide simply to comply with the existing regulations and processes and make adjustments as you need to. That's a completely appropriate choice depending on your team's capacity and status, and I encourage you to make it if it's the right one for you.

HOW LONG DOES ALL THIS TAKE?

Governments operate at broad scale, which can make it seem like development practices associated with scale in the private sector (like tightly coupled sprint and feedback cycles, a.k.a. Agile development) can be adopted wholesale. But these methods can be a trap for civic technologists, who often are dealing with situations where large scale and low practice maturity combine.

Implementing something like Agile with success relies on answering questions about what a product is for, how customers value it, and how the company measures success. Government agencies thinking of their work as *policy* don't typically need to address these *product* questions with the same urgency, and NGOs don't view themselves as competing for customers. Without those underlying answers, a method that depends on the entire team being able to collectively answer the question "What should we focus on to advance our core goal?" every two weeks—with the potential of being able to *shift* that goal on the table, no less—is going to be much harder.

So much of the speed in the private-sector tech industry is the result of preexisting work that has become a bit invisible. Consider all the steps that you'll have to complete to get to where you want to be:

- Does the agency already have a robust production environment? If not, you'll need to help them create one.
- Do they have strong testing and release processes?
- Does their tech stack support the kind of application you jointly want to build? If not, there's licensing, procurement, and possibly migration work ahead to get to one that does.
- For services that need to be available 24/7, is there a team structure in place to support and maintain it?
- Does the agency have the internal capacity to hire people outside its current job classes to sustain this into the future?
- What kind of assumptions does the existing process rest on? Have these ever been tested with whoever the users are?
- Is there a way to monitor the status or measure the success of a feature?

Then there's the reality that government has (as it should) fairly stringent security, accessibility, and language requirements; those will need to be addressed from the start.

We need judicious innovation; it's not reasonable to implement refined traffic analytics on a suite of websites that don't make the first page of a Google search, just as it's not reasonable to use A/B testing for minor copy changes on an app that only has a few thousand users. It may not be reasonable (okay, it's really not) to spin up a multidisciplinary agile team and start development sprints if there's still substantial strategic uncertainty. Even methods like going straight to prototype after user research rather than writing a report may not fit the environment in organizations where the preconditions aren't in place.

So how do you scale back on those expectations while still doing useful work? The good news is that there are lots of things you can accomplish in just weeks or months in the civic sphere, and many of those are the same things you could do in weeks or months in a private company. If you have good relationships, you can build a prototype. (You can also build a prototype without relationships, but I hope you won't, because you'll probably be disappointed with its impact.)

Let's consider another example. You can convert an important form from paper to digital; the technical and design work involved for this takes just a matter of hours. If you're the first to try such a conversion where you are, you can expect the process to be much slower initially because of the foundational work required to support online forms—but it tends to accelerate as people in the organization are exposed to it. Converting twenty or a hundred forms, as Josh Gee did in his two years with Boston, can be a major win.[8]

What else can you do in just a few weeks or months?

- You might be able to write and test an API
  or deploy a publicly available one.
- You can launch a landing page or create or redesign
  a small website; with the tools available in 2020,
  you can do this pretty quickly if it's urgent.[9]

You can do all of the above with a small team, and people will probably be impressed by your speed (which will help you gain the confidence of your partners). But most of these things don't, on their own, make a major and lasting impact.

If you want to make a significant positive impact on people's lives as a civic technologist, at some kind of scale, and you are starting from scratch, you should plan on a minimum of two years to see it through. Three to five years is more realistic in many situations—and even if you put in five years, there's no guarantee of success. This is as a core team

---

8 Gee, "What I Learned in Two Years of Moving Government Forms Online," Medium, February 22, 2018, https://medium.com/@jgee/what-i-learned-in-two-years-of-moving-government-forms-online-1edc4c2aa089.

9 States and cities with existing digital teams put up excellent informational websites about the COVID-19 pandemic in a matter of days, mainly by overtaxing their content and testing people temporarily. (But note: they already *had* content and testing people to begin with.)

member, where the work is your full-time job; you may also encounter some "spot" opportunities to consult with a team, where you can play a specialized role in a two-to-five year effort without spending the whole time in-house yourself.

BECOMING PART OF THE RELAY

Civic tech's particular role in this process brings new and important skills into the mix, but they are by no means the only valuable set of skills or perspectives. If we know the process will keep going even if we as individuals get exhausted and take breaks, then the two years or five years become less of a source of anxiety. Whatever you're able to contribute, for however long you're able to spend, will be valuable—especially if you write it down. Documentation is how you pass the baton in the relay.

If your project petered out after three years amid an administration change and a loss of funding (but might have had a shot to launch if you'd had access to users or a better relationship with legal partners), your analysis of what happened can give absolute wings to the next group to try it—and that's a huge contribution. If you work on one piece of a system that launches three years after you leave that particular agency, your contribution still mattered. If you tidy up the GitHub repo for the code your civic startup developed, as you shut the doors after eighteen months, you've left a precious artifact for someone to find. Getting an email thanking you, at a distance of years, will make your day like few other things—and people who do stewardship remember to do things like that.

• • •

So expect that it will take longer than private-sector projects. Expect that it will feel slower, and harder. But whether you succeed or fail in the short term, think of your work as part of the fifty-year project, and expect that your contribution will matter to some other person working on it. Make it easy to find, take a break if you need to, and come back when you're ready again.

CHAPTER 7

ESSENTIAL SKILLS

Civic technology can be the ideal means to put your tech skills to good use—but it will be your communication and collaboration skills that will clear the path for you to do that. Communicating well, managing through influence, and making good strategic choices are must-haves; everything from judgment to facilitation to persuasive writing is at a premium. There are not yet—and I'm not sure there ever should be—roles where you can have a major impact on the public good simply by quietly completing your tickets. You can expect to talk about your work, a lot— and to listen to other people talk about theirs.

In this chapter I'll discuss how to decide whether you have the skills for a particular civic tech challenge, and how to think about civic tech careers if you aren't already an experienced technologist. I'll also talk about key non-technical disciplines in the field, and the absolute requirement for strong communication and facilitation skills, whatever your technical specialty.

WHAT SKILLS DO YOU NEED TO SUCCEED IN CIVIC TECH?

I hear this question regularly. The simplest answer is that you need a combination of solid mid-level technology skills (in any discipline) with very strong communication skills, especially as a listener. If you can write clear pull requests, emails, or decks, present ideas and help facilitate meetings, then you have at least a baseline on the communications side. If you're also excited to understand new contexts and help others adapt your practices to them, then you have a good foundation to deploy those skills in change work.

It's not possible to succeed just by writing good code, designing beautiful flows, or writing well-crafted stories and epics (or, let's be real, business cases and schedules). But if you can do any of those things (or the many other technical possibilities—there's space for data scientists, content designers, system architects, tech-savvy lawyers, and more), then you're in the right ballpark on the technical side. A solid mid-level skill set in any engineering, design, or product discipline will generally mean you have the technology piece of what's needed to succeed in civic tech. And since the technology problems are rarely the most difficult part of a project, there are a lot of interesting spaces for people who have switched careers[1] and are more junior in their tech skill set but have expertise in other domains.

Apart from pinning down which sort of goal you're working toward, one of the most important decisions you need to make when identifying the projects you want to work on is which technical or organizational layer (or what part of the relevant "stack") you can most effectively work in to achieve that goal. This is a complement to figuring out where in the civic ecosystem the responsibility for it lives.

Websites present very interesting opportunities, because while the web interface is at a surface level of the stack, web projects have a way of exposing problems and opportunities at multiple levels, across multiple disciplines. Which will you tackle?

---

1 Legal and organizing skills are especially useful, but I've also seen budget experts, journalists, and public health workers achieve great things in civic tech.

- create new web content
- create new templates for the existing system
- revise or replace the system with a more flexible one
- integrate databases with a web publishing system for automated delivery of certain content
- reconfigure the program's data group and the IT teams to work more closely with one another

Any of these might demand a slightly different skill set—some more technical than others. And all of them are helpful when it comes to making a solid contribution to the field.

KNOW YOUR LIMITS: LEVELS OF COMPETENCE

I'm drafting this after the high-profile disaster of the Iowa caucus app in 2020. In the wake of the media meltdown, it became clear that the app was inadequately planned, tested, and supported; several experts came forward to say they would have refused the project or scoped it very differently, given the timeline and resources available.[2] A disaster under a national lens is everyone's nightmare, and reflects poorly on an entire field.

Having strength in your skill set is great, but what matters more than being the strongest data scientist in the field is that you know enough to know when you're out of your depth. Out of your depth is different from simply not knowing a particular thing. Out of your depth means you don't have the experience on which to form judgments about whether something is doable, or reasonable, or where the zones of risk are within a project.

It takes some insight to accurately rank your own competence at a given task. In the earliest stage of learning, a state sometimes called

---

2 Sara Morrison, "Iowa's 2016 Caucus App Worked and Everyone Forgot about It," Recode, Vox, February 7.2020, https://www.vox.com/recode/2020/2/7/21125078/iowa-caucus-2016-mobile-app-2020. Some compelling quotes from software developers here.

unconscious incompetence,[3] you aren't even aware of what you don't know. This often shows up in technology as learning the simple version of some task and then assuming a more complicated version will be easy. Basic competence learned from private-sector tech may give you a false sense of security when applying the same method to civic tech situations. For example, if you've done a few commercial usability studies, you might assume you know enough to get good information from a similar-length interview about an app interface for traumatized people seeking restraining orders. But a trauma-informed interview is much more complicated, and if you miss that, you can cause harm.

If you might still be in the "don't know what you don't know" stage of learning, you should work with senior partners and mentors. Feeling pretty sure that you know everything you need to know is a good sign that you're definitely still in this stage for at least some area of knowledge.

If you're safely over the hump into *conscious* incompetence (or "knowing what you don't know") while still learning, you're in a less risky stage, although you may feel constantly like you don't know enough. This feeling, while uncomfortable, is healthy. You might not have all the answers, but you have the critical ability to ask good questions, and to sound the alarm when you don't know if something is appropriately scoped or within the team's capacity. We all owe that to our partners and the public.

For most people at an intermediate level, mentors are still valuable. (And honestly, many seniors would love to have mentors too—they get harder and harder to come by as you advance.) As your own skill grows into conscious competence, you gain not only direct knowledge, but also a well-enough-developed "spidey sense" to evaluate your mentors. If you have grown your professional network to the point that you know who in your community can give reliable advice on issues where your skill set is weak, ideally not just from the dominant perspective, even better. That

---

3 On the four-stage model of competence, attributed to clinical psychologist Noel Burch (among others), see for example Linda Adams, "Learning a New Skill Is Easier Said than Done," Gordon Training International, n.d., https://www.gordontraining.com/free-workplace-articles/learning-a-new-skill-is-easier-said-than-done/.

ability to evaluate and source good advice will stand your team and your partners in good stead.

Even if you are very senior in your technology skills, watch out for areas of unconscious incompetence in a new context. Seniors have usually reached a level of *unconscious competence* where certain core skills have become habits and may even be difficult to explain. The strongest seniors continue to ask questions and entertain doubts, especially toward the edges of their skill set. And, most important, they continue to recognize their own limits and can help more junior people see theirs.

FRAMEWORKS AND FLEXIBILITY

If you are an engineer, you may wonder which languages or frameworks will be most useful—and this is a difficult question. Many government organizations have standardized on Oracle or Microsoft products across much of their technology stack, so familiarity with some of those enterprise suites and their associated languages is often helpful (and gives you an easy path to credibility with partners)—but if you're building a website, which will be part of many projects, it doesn't have to be the whole story.

One hallmark of the past decade in the tech industry was a commitment to methods and tools. Whether it was Agile, Lean, Design Thinking, or DevOps (and DesignOps and ResearchOps), software teams thought and talked about process a whole lot. A whole universe of productivity tools geared toward these methods came to market. Most of us were convinced that our preferred method had many advantages if we could just get everyone to do it right. A lot of us, probably correctly, attribute our success in shipping software at least partly to some combination of methods and tools. One of the most obvious moves we can make in the civic space is to implement the methods and tools we know work.

That said, a flexible attitude about specific methods and tools is most productive. Processes and tools that were designed for high-resource environments to maximize financial outcomes won't necessarily suit low-resourced projects with huge mission goals.

In general terms, it's more helpful to be familiar with stable technology stacks than with the very latest ones. In my best estimation, it will be a number of years before the basic building blocks of networked computing, databases, and the mobile web will be out of the core set. To take one example, if you are strong in JavaScript, and somewhat agnostic as to the specific front-end framework your team works in—perhaps even able to help your partners compare the strengths of several for their situation—you will have a very useful capability set for doing civic work as a front-end engineer.

And whatever parts of the stack you work in, having confidence to learn and adopt the preferred stack of likely partners will also serve you well. If you find someone in the IT or web or analyst group who is interested in working with you, the best way to lean into that partnership may be to adopt their language of choice and focus your coaching on the collaborative and iterative aspects of modern practices.

But all that said, there is much to bring along from the private-sector methods you're expert in. The key is to treat them as flexible models rather than rigid templates, and to ask yourself and your team questions like these:

- Which parts of an Agile process will help us with the goals we're working on?
- Do we have the prerequisites for good UX practice and, if not, how easy will it be to acquire them?

This is a great arena in which to pick your battles carefully. In many cases, the pain of acquiring Trello for a government team will be much higher than of simply managing tasks in a spreadsheet. Likewise, the friction of getting people bought in to video meetings, and equipping them for it, will often be much higher than using conference calls on Polycoms. Being flexible about tools means you may need to adapt your preferred style of getting work done—something I'll say even more about in Chapter 11.

NOT-STRICTLY-TECH WORK IN CIVIC TECH

In thinking about your own experience, skills that might not be centered on a technology résumé could be extremely useful in civic projects. Have you:

- run budgets?
- written job descriptions?
- testified at a community meeting?
- managed grants?
- worked on or with purchasing at a larger company?
- set standards or worked with standards bodies?
- participated in campaigns or other organizing efforts?
- met with policymakers or sat on committees?
- practiced law?

Any of these "non-tech" experiences will be valuable in working to help public-sector groups better serve their constituents using technology.

People who focus on policies, regulations, budgets, procurement, and other operational needs are essential to getting work done in the public sector. A law degree or a history of nonprofit work is an underrated path for entering civic tech. People who begin with experience in these areas and go on to acquire tech skills on top of that[4] often make great things happen.

Some government groups go so far as to have designated "bureaucracy hackers" who are responsible for helping clear a path for technology work. In one famous effort, staff at the United States Digital Service decided to spend the time to actually read the technology sections of the Federal Acquisition Regulations—a two-thousand-plus page compendium of rules about purchasing and procurement—and create a shorter, more accessible guide to rules about technology.[5]

---

4 Think accessible, practical skills—user research or content design if you have a journalism background, or data science if you have a background in statistics.

5 United States Digital Service, "The TechFAR Handbook," https://playbook.cio.gov/techfar/.

Work along these lines—whether it's writing such a guide, making privacy requirements transparent, or identifying a purchasing authority that offers options for buying essential services—may be some of the most impactful work a project can offer. If you have the skills to do so, consider them among your top qualifications.

IF YOU'RE STARTING YOUR CAREER

Civic tech is a tough space for true juniors and new graduates, but more and more apprenticeships and other developmental programs are starting to crop up. Many organizations consider the ability to onboard, mentor, and advance juniors to be a meaningful way to gauge the health of a technology group. I agree with them. Doing it well requires dedicating significant organizational capacity to a long-term goal, which means you have to be operating with a comfortable abundance of time and resources.

I want to be honest about the state of the field as it now stands. If you're looking for a first job with the intention of going into civic tech, look for a team that operates with healthy levels of resources. Ask for details about how you'll be trained and mentored and how they'll evaluate your growth. If they have good answers, that indicates you'll get the support you need, and that there's probably room for advancement.

However, many government technology groups are not operating in a healthy state of abundance at all. Supporting juniors badly tends to mean the juniors get neither the learning nor the career advancement they hope for. And if the tech instruction isn't as solid as it would be in a more tech-oriented space, or if the senior people are too overworked to properly mentor, juniors may end up without a clear understanding of their skill level, and with fewer options for transferring back to industry.

I worry that without the careful design of programs,[6] juniors' technical growth from entry-level civic tech jobs will at best be equivalent to any

---

6 As of 2020, there are a couple of civic tech organizations (Code for America and Nava PBC) that have announced apprenticeship programs; to my mind, these formal programs from values-driven groups are likely to deliver the kind of experience juniors deserve.

entry-level tech job. If that's true, there's a strong case to be made for taking a higher-paid job in mainstream tech for a period of time, because the effects of early salary levels compound over a career.[7]

The best way to prepare for a civic tech career is to learn as much as you can about different methods, value systems, and types of constraints, and to refine your collaboration skills by working with as many different types of people as possible. If you find an opportunity to do some of that by joining a well-structured program run by a civic tech company, go for it! But know that if you don't find that, you can prepare just as well by honing your skills in your technology discipline and participating in civic life in any way that is accessible to you.

And working at a traditional technology company, especially one big enough to have a strong perspective on practice, will teach you valuable skills if you have that opportunity. Get used to thinking about the value systems and power dynamics embedded in both enterprises, and where technology does or doesn't make sense as a piece of the puzzle. Watch groups of people collaborate in healthy and unhealthy ways, and develop a perspective on how to collaborate well. Refine some basic digital technology skill set (this can even be web writing or spreadsheets) to the point where you could teach it to others. You will be ready to enrich the field when you do join formally—and it's on those of us who are already here to make sure there is more and more opportunity by the time you do join us.

• • •

As in almost every project area, people who are senior enough to have developed a strong perspective on their discipline and a flexible toolbox of methods are extremely valuable. They can mentor junior civic technologists and interested partners, represent new practices to leadership teams effectively, and lead a team in scoping and solving

---

7 Particularly if you are a woman or a person of color (or both), setting an industry salary baseline for yourself may allow you more negotiation space later in your career.

problems. One or two very experienced people can provide perspective for a whole team of more junior designers or developers, and this is a model that can work across skill sets.

Just as one or two experienced bureaucrats can help fifty technologists understand their regulatory obligations and government structures, so can one or two experienced product managers help a large government group learn how to think about their services as products.

If you're a mid-level private-sector technologist, there's almost certainly a specialty where "a strong perspective and a flexible toolbox" describes you. And there's almost certainly a need for that specialty in the public sector—as well as for someone to champion, adapt, and support it.

If you have the communication skills and the curiosity to go along with it, you are ready. We need people at all experience levels, appropriately supported, to get this done.

CHAPTER 8

PROJECT TEAMS AND METHODS

As of 2020, most civic tech work is also *change work*: it aims not just to build software that meets the public's needs, but to increase the capacity of the public sector to do so. That means introducing new practices and shifting some of those in place, while respecting and supporting public-sector values. Government project teams are usually organized differently from private-sector teams; adaptability is a critical value for civic technologists to meet their partners where they are when introducing and adapting methods from the private sector to new contexts.

Depending on whether you join a government or volunteer project, you will likely encounter two different sets of assumptions about how to use technology to achieve goals. One is hierarchical and belongs to "IT" (as opposed to "tech") groups inside mission organizations, and sometimes extends to vendors who work with them. It assumes that technology is a separate and subordinate area to the "program" or "mission" work, focused purely on execution of requirements. The other belongs to open-source software projects and is self-consciously "flat" (non-hierarchical), with high value on public demonstrations of technical merit and an assumption that technical contributors are at least equal to business- or design-oriented members of the project.

When you start a civic tech project, you'll want to be able to identify partners who work on the same things you do—and they may have different titles than you'd expect. You may need to coach people, possibly very senior people, and to explain things that you've taken for granted for years—and you'll need to understand things that are completely alien to you in turn. You may also need to work to even access people who can give you needed data or resources. Using "soft skills" to this degree is taxing even for people who consider communication their primary skill set. Expect a fair amount of your energy to go into this kind of work, but take heart: as long as you're learning, none of the effort will be wasted.

GOVERNMENT TEAMS AND ASSUMPTIONS

To the extent that government builds (rather than buys) software, the groups that do it are found in information technology (IT) departments.[1] The people dealing with code will typically be called "application developers" or "IT analysts" rather than engineers. There will be staff members called something like "business systems analysts" who own some of the responsibilities you're used to product management and UX groups handling under a different name, and often with strikingly different assumptions.

It's very unusual for there to be product managers in IT departments, at least not as they're thought of in groups that identify as "tech" instead—although in groups that have adopted some version of Agile practice, there may be people called "product owners". And there will definitely be both program and project managers, but they may not be part of the IT department.

---

1 This will be the bulk of the technology staff, even if there's an innovation lab or digital service team in place.

One thing you'll find is a bright distinction between program staff and IT staff, usually with a fairly formal request process when program staff want to do technology work. While the titles and some of the expectations may be different, all of these people are critical colleagues.

Even though most governments have some internal tech capacity, there's very likely to be at least one vendor working on any given project. They may be there for user research, design,[2] build capacity that the internal team doesn't have, system integration, or consulting on some particular software stack or technical problem. Technical vendors will most likely report to the IT team, but program staff may sometimes directly contract with design or research vendors.

These companies and the people who work for them are also essential colleagues, but it can be hard to connect with them. Some vendor contracts are structured for "go away and take care of this" work, and some overworked government clients assume that's the model that will cause them the least stress. Making things more collaborative means working across all the in-house and vendor groups as much as you can, and if you're on the vendor side yourself, structuring your proposal to make that possible in the contract.[3]

OPEN-SOURCE TEAMS AND ASSUMPTIONS

If you join a group that works outside government on the volunteer or start-up side of civic tech, you may instead encounter the roles and practices common to open-source projects. This will often be a more engineering-centric experience, although civic tech groups have worked hard to welcome and support design colleagues over the last several years. It's very likely that such a group will make heavy use of online shared repositories like GitHub, and will follow the processes that those

---

2 Research and design vendors are both quite common, since few government agencies carry a UX or digital design role, and most have challenging internal rules about paying participant incentives for research studies.

3 Colocation, even part-time, can be great for this, and frequent status meetings (call them stand-ups or not) are a must.

embody, so it's well worth becoming familiar with them. Most of the people participating in a project like this will be familiar with the engineering-design-product triad and many will be eager to work with you, whichever slot you fit in.

THE ENGINEERING-DESIGN-PRODUCT TRIAD

Most private-sector technology teams in the 2010s, whether at a major company or a start-up, divided software responsibilities into three broad buckets: engineering, design, and product. Engineering often outnumbers the other two by a factor of ten or more, but they are all considered key components of the process. Most large-scale civic tech projects also adopt this three-way division, and with it the Agile-derived concept of *self-organizing teams* where people from all three disciplines collaborate to achieve clear goals without micromanagement from above.

There's more to each category, of course. Design may include a research group, a UX group, a visual group, a content group, and possibly even a service design group.[4] Engineering includes back-end, front-end, security, DevOps, testing, data science, and more. Product is typically the smallest and least likely to be subdivided into multiple disciplines.

The success of the engineering-design-product triad depends on a few things that would be typical of a high-resourced private-sector organization with some market experience behind it:

- Everyone shares an understanding of the goal.
- It's clear how technology can be used to achieve the goal.
- At least some of the ecosystem and architecture challenges are already known.

If these foundations aren't solid, then starting to churn through sprints, or design and build against a plan, will only result in wasted resources and angry partners.

---

4 The term "service design" is more common in Europe, especially for government design, and the practice implies permission to work on non-digital touchpoints as well as software.

The traditional three-way division of responsibilities with close collaboration is productive in software build teams and has strengths in civic tech, but can offer some pitfalls when software build isn't the primary goal. More worryingly, practitioners' comfort with it can lead to an assumption that it fits all situations, or even that software build is the right approach to every problem. If you discover instead that training content authors, or intervening in a procurement process, is the best avenue for your team to do good right now, then a team mostly staffed with engineers or UI designers will need flexibility to move forward.

The question of where in the technical or organizational stack to invest a team's efforts in order to deliver the most value to the most users and stakeholders is exactly the kind of strategic product decision that benefits from a product skill set and mindset. Because there are many problems that good software can't solve (and many more where it will only succeed after other kinds of work have been done), the lack of strategic product management can slow or confuse any number of initiatives in civic tech. Civic tech product people who work inside institutions spend a lot of their time coaching and helping build the mindset to make these decisions well.

LEVELING UP PARTNER TEAMS

Despite government's reputation for requiring a million sign-offs to correct a typo on a website, I've often found that when it comes to the push to production, processes can be shockingly informal. Production monitoring may be nonexistent; quality assurance (QA) may be quite informal and not present as an organizational group. (It's surprising to me, as someone who spent several years of my tech career in QA, that civic tech doesn't have more strength in that discipline as well. I would love to see more QA jobs in some of our mature teams.) If this is the situation where you are, you will definitely need to befriend and persuade an IT group to set up even the precursors to a DevOps practice. The same goes for Agile or other iterative development models.

Assuming you want to improve release discipline and velocity, reduce bugs and outages, and make code more maintainable for the next people to work on it, you will need to effect change in a whole range of processes. Cleaner, more modern software always seems desirable—but only to the extent that its champions also offer the capacity to maintain it and sustain continuous improvement into the future. Many technical people argue that cutting-edge software isn't as useful as solid software built on one-generation-back architectures and languages.

So let's say you want to get to better, more stable, or faster software, without taking on changes in service goals. You are probably looking at a whole lot of persuasion and coordination work. It's worth noting that methods evolve out of specific conditions, and the conditions you find in the public sector may or may not replicate the ones you've seen in private-sector tech. If your experience is heavily influenced by metrics and optimization goals and other established tech methods, you may find that your agency is at too early a maturity level even to collect useful quantitative data. If your experience is tilted toward start-ups, where speed is of the essence and many trade-offs will be easily resolved in favor of moving faster to maximize runway, you may find that factors like access and budget timing weigh much heavier in public-sector work.

You may be tempted to grab the well-documented Spotify team organization[5] as a touchstone, or a government-friendly framework like Scaled Agile Framework (SAFe),[6] but it's well worth stopping to assess whether your team is mature enough to make the jump. If it's not, figure out which aspect of modern software development is the most likely to show results and start with that. Treat it as a bit of a meta-sprint. Remember that every change you push means someone has to deal with a disruption of their work—so make sure you make it worth it for them.

---

5 Spotify's model enjoyed a long run of popularity, but has recently come under some heavy scrutiny. See Henrik Kniberg and Anders Ivarsson, "Scaling Agility @ Spotify with Tribes, Squads, Chapters & Guilds," Crisp's Blog, October 2012, https://blog.crisp.se/wp-content/uploads/2012/11/SpotifyScaling.pdf; and Jeremiah Lee, "Failed @SquadGoals," April 19, 2020, https://www.jeremiahlee.com/posts/failed-squad-goals/.

6 SAFe was designed as an enterprise-friendly adaptation of Agile and is relatively common in government organizations (https://www.scaledagileframework.com/).

FILLING IN FOR PRODUCT MANAGEMENT

In my experience, the private-sector discipline that is most underdeveloped in government is product management. I don't just mean the disempowered version where someone with a "product" title is in charge of a backlog, but the strategic discipline of uniting a team around a product vision and making trade-offs across technical, design, and business domains to determine how to invest and when to ship. In assessing the overall value delivered to the public, it's not sufficient to aim for better, faster software—it needs to be *useful* to its audience.

Product management is also the hardest "tech" skill to translate directly to a space that doesn't think of itself as making, well, products. Product owner roles, reduced to a person who runs meetings and grooms the backlog, are relatively easy to find, but product management as it's practiced in the best Silicon Valley groups is almost from another planet. If you're used to working with strong product management in this mode, you will likely miss it very much and will see the usefulness of bringing a product management mindset in to complement improvements in engineering.

This is a real challenge. "Program management" is a familiar term and practice in government, but it's very different.[7] Most government processes assume that software is specified by internal groups of business analysts brainstorming together and then built, probably by a vendor, and that the builders are working for the specifiers. There isn't a market per se, so market analysis isn't really relevant, and goals are much less likely to include concrete value delivered to users. But you can take advantage of public servants' strong motivation to deliver value to the public, and show how software can be thought of as a flexible means to that end.[8]

---

7 "Program manager" usually means a higher-level project manager with a portfolio of projects that they must keep in alignment.

8 Product management isn't as prolific in books or conferences as design or engineering, but in recent years the international Mind the Product organization has been a strong center for training and conversation (https://www.mindtheproduct.com).

• • •

One of the most important soft skills you need alongside your solid tech abilities is the ability to identify yourself as a fellow traveler to the colleagues who may be working under different names or titles, and learn from them at least as much as you teach. If you can recognize the person who does complicated formula work in Excel as someone doing programming, or the person who revises form letters as someone who makes user-centered design decisions, you'll be able to treat them as peers and show them all the parts of your practice and community that can make their work easier. Meanwhile, what you find out about the challenges they face and the goals they're pursuing will make you better at civic tech, and for most people, an outright better technologist.

CHAPTER 9

WORKING WITH POLICY

Public policy is an entire field and practice with a wealth of literature and many experts in academia and government. Many technologists—myself included—don't come to civic tech with any policy training or experience, apart from interactions with company policies related to time off or travel that are equivalent to "rules."

Policy, in its most specific definition, is a particular administration or agency's interpretation of how to apply laws and regulations. On the spectrum of government control from most formal (laws, then regulations) to least formal (guidance[1]), policy sits in the middle.

A second important meaning of *policy* is broader, basically meaning "the ways government solves a problem or accomplishes a goal." This includes whether agencies or elected officials choose to pursue a specific goal (active) or ignore an issue (passive)—either way, it's still policy. When

---

1 Though less formal, you can still get in trouble as a government worker if you don't follow guidance (or suggestions for the right ways agencies ought to comply)—but it's not the same level of trouble you can get in for not following the law.

political candidates discuss different policies, it's usually in this sense of the word.

So where do technologists fit in the landscape of policy? It's not something we can pick up quickly at an expert level. Good software and good systems are important, but there are limits to what they can do on their own. Most significantly, they can't change policy goals or compensate for overly complicated policy. Where can we usefully support and influence colleagues who come to public-sector work from a policy perspective?

HOW POLICY EVOLVES IN PRACTICE

The policy landscape can be complicated. Yet understanding both the relevant policy goals of the administration you're working under and the explicit formal and informal instructions embedded in policy and guidance is critical. Having a sense of the policy landscape helps you understand your constraints and estimate the level of effort you may need to change something that can't be addressed through technology. For example, a statutory change will be a very significant effort and is usually beyond the reach of civic tech initiatives, whereas new policy or guidance might be achievable with just a solid amount of in-agency persuasion and proposal.

Let's look at an active area of policy change to illustrate some of this. In 1995, marijuana was illegal for all purposes throughout the United States, but penalties for possession and use were different in different locations. Beginning in the 1970s, a few cities and states had pursued a policy of decriminalization, reducing the official consequences for some levels of illegal activity. In the 1990s, San Francisco Mayor Willie Brown explicitly made cannabis enforcement the last priority of the police department. So while it was technically illegal to light up on a street corner, in practice a fair number of people felt safe doing it. This made San Francisco very different from cities where strict enforcement policies existed at all levels of government. However, even in San Francisco, if you were investigated by the federal Drug Enforcement Agency, which had (and still has even in

2020) a policy of strong enforcement, the local policy of lenience would not help you.

From 1996 to 2018, multiple states passed laws legalizing cannabis use for medical purposes. Regulations associated with these laws set up rules and licensing systems for both dispensaries and patients. Most of the time, federal authorities have chosen a policy of noninterference with these systems, although federal law remains unchanged. But the conflict remains: you can still fail a federal background check for cannabis use, even if you have a medical card from your state.

In 2020, the legal and policy landscape is even more complicated. Several states have fully legalized adult use of marijuana, including recreational use, while others allow medical use with varying formality of doctor's recommendation required; a few maintain their 1995 status quo. As states have legitimized cannabis, a whole thicket of policy questions has emerged. For example:

- Should past marijuana convictions be expunged from people's records? If so, how?
- Can we create opportunities for the populations that bore the brunt of enforcement to participate in the legal marijuana business under the new licenses?
- How should cannabis growers and manufacturers sell their products to customers? Are independent stores allowed? Is delivery allowed?
- What kind of enforcement should there be for breaking rules?

Trained policymakers answer questions like these through a canonical process cycle encompassing development,[2] implementation, and evaluation. In many ways, the cycle is similar to the build/measure/learn feedback loop from Lean methodology, but more formal and with different assumptions about how and how fast changes occur. While policy development is something of a negotiation between legislative and executive branches, policy implementation and evaluation are largely the province of the executive branch, with oversight from the legislature.

---

2 The development stage is often broken into agenda-setting and formulation substages.

Outcomes and *interventions* are important terms for policy development that play the same role "goal" and "hypothesis" do if you're used to an Agile/Lean technology framework. For example, if we want to attract more businesses to our downtown district (outcome/goal), we might do it by offering a tax incentive (intervention/hypothesis).

Most governments implement most policy through executive-branch programs, with explicit funding through the legislative budget process. Programs can be designed to achieve specific policy outcomes via policy interventions. On a local level, these outcomes might include goals like fewer people who are food insecure, more houses that meet storm-safety code, or a stronger local business sector; outcomes on the national level might be broader, like more or fewer immigrants, or more people going to college.

People with expertise in metrics and evaluation will look at the success of a given intervention and a policy as a whole. Evaluation groups are always part of the structure of accountability to the legislature. Evaluation can reveal successes and failures, and may generate new problems to be solved with policy levers. If you're a data scientist, a product manager, or a user researcher, make it an immediate priority to meet the nearest evaluation group and learn what they're up to. They're likely to be doing rigorous, academic-style research on questions related to the ones you're looking at in a shorter-term, less formal frame. Their work can definitely inform yours, and yours might well be able to inform theirs.

POLICY IMPLEMENTATION
IS THE BIGGEST OPPORTUNITY FOR TECH

Most technologists in government end up working on the policy implementation stage of the development–implementation–evaluation cycle. If you find some of the above questions about cannabis policy compelling, then working with policymakers might be a good fit for you. A state or municipality can take many approaches to each of these questions, and which one wins will depend on the policy objectives and preferred policy levers of the stakeholders.

Policy *levers* are just the means of achieving policy outcomes, without being as specific about which intervention is applied in a particular case. Levers may include incentives, penalties, rules, nudges, and many more possibilities; but their effectiveness is always going to depend on how well they are implemented. This is where technology plays its biggest role.

Jennifer Pahlka, the founder of Code for America, calls situations where policy is fully formed but processes, tools, or interfaces are inhibiting its success "the implementation gap." Engaging with exactly these situations—and there are thousands, so the opportunity is almost boundless—is a great way for technologists to use our specific skills while respecting the expertise of people who have made public policy their life's work. Finding places where better technology implementations have potential to make policies successful is a winner on a number of levels.

In our cannabis example, a policy of expunging past marijuana convictions has several parts where technology could be important to the implementation. Start with finding records that meet criteria; that's database work. Maybe this process is kicked off by someone applying for expungement; in that case, it will need a public-facing UI. Or maybe the process is automatic; that would mean more complicated database search and engineering. If the process has an approval step involving district attorneys, that would mean a different UI for a different, professional public. Maybe it needs a confirmation step with a message sent to either people with past convictions or background-check providers or both; this would mean system integration and service design.

And all of this is just a start. Technology groups are doing exactly this kind of work in several cities where governments want to mass-expunge past marijuana records. While the success of the policy may not be entirely dependent on technology, it's easy to see that poor software or design implementations could derail it, and excellent ones could further it.

That being said, there is very little technology can do to address these questions if expungement is not the adopted policy of the right government entities—which is why it's really important to understand the nuances of where a policy stands in order to see where technology can work with it. For example, imagine you're working on technological solutions to help reduce excess or redundant fees levied by an agency onto the public.

- If your partner agency has an explicit policy of never reducing fees, your best design for an eligibility checker for fee reduction can't be more than a thought experiment.
- If the agency has a disused policy about fee reduction in some circumstances that isn't strongly implemented, and unclear guidance to frontline workers about it, with the effect that it almost never reduces anyone's fees, there's more room for a combination of technical and collaborative work to make a difference. Your first step in this case is asking questions.
- If your agency has a clear policy that fee reductions for eligible users are favored, and clear guidance to frontline workers to process fee-reduction eligibility as a priority, but the forms and process used to do so are cumbersome, you have a huge opportunity.
- If your agency has a new administrator who is excited to reduce fees for as many eligible people as possible, then you have an ideal partner, but you may not actually be in as strong a position as in the previous example if the policy pieces aren't in place. You may be able to start in parallel with a policy effort and offer iterative demos along the way, but it's a little bit less of a slam dunk.

HOW CAN TECH METHODS APPLY?

Once you're interested in policy and its potential for problem-solving, you may wonder if methods more familiar to you would help. Tech is problem-solving too, after all. And there are parts of the policy cycle where human-centered design methods and rapid prototyping in particular can be useful.

Policy development has historically been a top-down endeavor conducted by highly educated experts in highly placed positions. It has reflected the typically hierarchical structure of government, with implementation seen as second-stage—and sometimes lower-status—work, with a pretty hard handoff between the two. This will sound familiar to people who have worked in waterfall technology processes, where there's a handoff from planning to design to execution.

While you shouldn't assume that all expert policymaking needs an overhaul, the top-down approach has some of the same pitfalls that big-release software processes do. Big policy changes can be just as high-risk as big software system cutovers. In particular, where policies are designed to benefit specific groups of people, but the designers aren't members of those communities, the same problems will crop up as when software design teams don't understand their users or have sufficient diversity. And when policy interventions are intended to influence individual behavior at scale, then a top-down, big-release process rests on a lot of assumptions and introduces a high level of risk.

Policy schools and programs are beginning to adopt and adapt methods from human-centered design for some of these situations, especially for testing and iterating policy designs.[3] Led by these efforts, it makes sense for technologists to bring methods like rapid prototyping and user research to help with policy design stages if opportunities arise. Paper or digital prototyping, as a way to make ideas concrete in refining a policy design, can be especially useful.

Prototypes built for policy processes should be explicitly throw-away products—and you should actively plan for how they will be tested with constituents and how they will be thrown away, so they don't end up getting pressed into production uses they were never intended for

We've known for some time that these methods can be useful for more than software. That said, it's not uncommon for techies to think our toolbox is the most useful and to want to substitute it for every other set of tools we encounter. But it isn't better; the tools are just designed for different goals, and they have their own pitfalls. Bringing knowledge of where they may fit imperfectly (for example, the 2010s tech toolbox's focus on commercial growth) is important if you get to participate in a policy process. It's

---

3 In 2020, Harvard's Kennedy School of Government even has more than one methods class taught by civic designers.

important to model and reinforce that consciousness and maintain an adaptive attitude to the work; fixed adherence to your preferred methods tends to make for more brittle solutions that may struggle to respond adaptively to future changes.

TECHNOLOGY POLICY

The area where technologists have major potential to influence new policy development is (perhaps unsurprisingly) in policy related to technology matters. How an institution uses technology is not just the result of technology and design decisions; it's set by all kinds of policy decisions.

For example, in the court system, *rules of court* govern whether and how parties can appear in court remotely. Video technology has existed for a long time, but it can't just be deployed. Many courts had to shut down during the COVID quarantine, and in order to bring some hearings back on emergency status, they didn't just have to set up videoconference systems—they had to get an emergency change to the rules of court. If you favor video appearances as an access-to-justice measure, you would have to work on a permanent rule change as well as a viable technology proposal. But if you're an experienced technologist with the right relationships, you might be very well positioned to advocate for such a change.

How members of the public may or may not use technology to access services and public meetings and perform civic duties is a policy issue as much as a technology issue. Voting methods are another fantastic example. What's the right way to maximize voter participation (if that's indeed a goal of the Secretary of State), correctly record all voters' intent, be sure of the results quickly, and have auditable records, all without overtaxing local election departments' resources?

States and counties jointly administer US elections, so there's no one office to make a single choice about voting tech for the whole country. Vote-by-mail has become increasingly popular in the US over the past decade. Events like Hurricane Sandy in 2012 and the COVID pandemic in 2020 disrupted traditional in-person voting, and the Supreme Court's ruling against part of the Voting Rights Act in 2013 led to long lines to vote in Black communities in every election since. Policymakers charged with ensuring fair elections need answers.

Technology has a part to play in answering that policy question, and it's in everyone's interest for policymakers to understand its potential and its pitfalls. Vote-by-mail *sounds* low-tech, but in reality it involves complicated mapping, printing, verification, and tracking elements. Tech people can help sort out the strengths of vote-by-mail versus in-person voting by machine versus online options—but, crucially, only if those tech people are well versed in election administration issues.

Technologists can also influence infrastructural digital policy like how governments support high-speed, affordable broadband connectivity or how the dot-gov domain registry works. In the 1990s, dot-gov domains were hard to use because of restrictive policies about outbound links to non-dot-gov domains. Many local governments preferred to avoid them because they wanted to link to private or NGO resources. (If your city or town has a dot-com or dot-org website, this is why.) In the 2000s, technologists advising the dot-gov registry changed this and standardized rules for local government web addresses in order to help "regular" people understand whether they're on a legitimate government site. At any government level, advising on similarly complex rules about API access to government systems, or on requirements for authority to operate, will be in many technical people's wheelhouse.

POLICY EXCEPTIONS AND CHANGE

While early stages of a technology initiative (for example, an innovation lab that mainly builds prototypes) can sometimes put aside questions of policy, in later stages the policy needs to align to support the continuation of the work. Understanding how policy works internally is important for future-proofing projects. It's possible, even likely, that your initial partnership with a particular government entity (whether you're a volunteer, a contractor, or an employee) is enabled by an exception or an area of flexibility in standard policy. Such spots of flexibility are often temporary—discretionary exceptions are exactly the things that a newer administrator can reverse quickly if their priorities are different. (And they sometimes do, just to show there's a new sheriff in town.)

If a civic tech project has been enabled by special hiring, what will it take to allow the department to hire those sorts of people more permanently, as part of its ordinary HR structure? If it rests on data released as a pilot, what will it take to make sure that data keeps being available and up to date? What would it take to make more such releases possible? If a policy intervention shows promise from an early tech success, is there a way that the policy process can support that intervention more formally? Because civic tech work is always also change work, these are questions that you should grow your capacity to work on if you want to make an impact.

• • •

Policy is an unfamiliar landscape for many technologists, but even if you're not a policy expert, you have likely gained experience in different policy environments—whether in different agencies or government levels, or even in the private sector. Analyzing those experiences can help you articulate the effects of a restrictive policy compared to one that's more open. You may, for example, be able to explain the ins and outs of open-source software for a department that's considering a policy intervention of open-sourcing certain kinds of code by default to allow public review. Or if you are a designer, you might work out an equitable framework for user research recruitment and compensation that could be implemented via policy on payments to constituents.

Techies are often tempted to tackle unfamiliar territory with the tools we feel most comfortable using. But policy is an area where we need to respect the expertise (and the tools) of policy partners, even as we offer to help. This is one of the most interesting learning opportunities in civic tech. Even as we think about ways to make the loop between policy, service design, and actual code shorter, policy thinking offers us one of the best ways to understand the problems we're here to help solve

CHAPTER 10

MAKING LONG-TERM CHANGE

Over the past decade, as more and more technologists have shared what they've learned, a few civic tech projects have stood out as being particularly fruitful for lasting change, while others have been brittle or short-lived. What's the crucial factor for bigger and more lasting impact? We're still working that out, but it's clear that two projects with very similar short-term goals and methods can have completely different outcomes. Some projects leave a government or civic agency significantly more capable of using tech to serve the public; others don't do much beyond a software launch. There can be a number of reasons for that.

We've just learned about policy and the need to understand the land-scape, and that's great—but we're here to make concrete improvements and we want those changes to last. We need to find ways to influence *practice* in directions that begin to make openness and responsiveness a new default. So where can we be most effective?

In this chapter, I'll introduce several areas where you can amplify your efforts and make your projects more likely to lead to change on a transformative scale. All of them are difficult, and all have limits, but it's hard to achieve more than a transient success without paying attention to some of them; a strong civic technologist in the 2020s should at least be aware of the outlines of these core areas of work.

OPEN DATA

Municipal civic tech in the United States has been heavily influenced by the idea of government as a platform.[1] In this framework, government should open its doors and make room for a competitive marketplace of services and interfaces built on solid, verified government data.

It's a compelling idea, especially to technologists, and it merged quickly into an already operational area of work that aimed to make government data public for transparency and accountability reasons. Dozens of municipalities have created open-data portals in the past decade on the theory that "if you build it, they will come"—*they* being technologists and start-ups eager to build great experiences for constituents.

A few spectacular early hits—like opening transit data with the General Transit Feed Specification (GTFS) standard,[2] leading to all the "when is my train coming" apps so appreciated by urban dwellers—produced a flurry of attempts to recreate these successes. Between 2011 and 2014, hundreds of public hackathons held in city halls aimed to create apps based on public data. We began to see a whole ecosystem of private apps making use of public data to deliver a choice of experiences to the public—particularly in the areas of transit and weather.

Many people in the civic tech community put substantial effort into pushing governments to release more data and allow more interaction

---

1 This comes from a 2010 Tim O'Reilly article in which he proposes that government invite public participation not just in deliberative processes but in building the ways government serves and interacts with the public. See O'Reilly, "Government as a Platform," *innovations* 6, no. 1 (2010): 13–40, https://www.mitpressjournals.org/doi/pdf/10.1162/INOV_a_00056.

2 One of the creators of the standard wrote about its history in a 2013 Code for America book. See Bibiana McHugh, "Pioneering Open Data Standards: The GTFS Story," in Beyond Transparency, eds. Brett Goldstein and Lauren Dyson (Code for America Press, 2013), https://beyondtransparency.org/part-2/pioneering-open-data-standards-the-gtfs-story/.

with their systems. As of 2020, we have a wealth of data available for journalists and coders to use; but we don't exactly have the vibrant marketplace of government service options that people expected ten years ago. As civic tech matures, we're slowly recognizing that open data and skilled people aren't all it takes.

It turns out that cleaning, standardizing, and maintaining datasets is a lot of work, with additional effort sometimes required to make them publicly valuable. San Francisco's data department learned this about food-inspection scores. They found that no one will really use a standalone app for restaurant inspection scores, but when the department set up a multi-sided partnership where Yelp consumed inspection-score data from an API and displayed it alongside reviews, users of *that* app found it valuable.

Making the best use of data requires product management vision, connections within government, and a plan for long-term sustainability of both the data and whatever is built on top of it. If a useful application requires integrating data from multiple agencies, then the coordination work escalates apace. Lots of coordination doesn't mean something isn't worth doing—there would be no civic tech if that were true. But to make the case that opening a particular dataset (or a whole group of datasets) will serve a government's mission, we need some accounting for how much work it will be to keep it up to date.

The good news is that agencies that have opened their datasets are often open to collaboration as well, so even if the full government-as-a-platform vision doesn't materialize, open data makes a strong starting point for deeper partnership.

IMPROVING PROCUREMENT

Procurement, as we saw in chapter 6, is a major area of regulation in government work—often maddeningly so. If it weren't essential for governments to be able to get good technology services, it would be tempting to recommend leaving procurement alone. But the problem is so embedded in the challenges of government tech, and it's so rare that a project doesn't need some kind of vendor help, that we have to work on it.

There are a number of efforts to improve the situation, from 18F Acquisition's templated processes and handbooks for federal procurement, to SmartProcure and CoProcure,[3] to the State Software Collaborative, a state-level cooperative purchasing and maintenance project convened by the Beeck Center at Georgetown.

Better, simpler documents are the clearest answer to better major procurements. Helping to write RFIs, RFPs, and evaluation criteria is a great thing to do if you're allowed to; streamlining them where possible is important. (Sometimes contracting departments add legal language after each contract problem they have, ending up with the fine-print equivalent of spaghetti code.) Make it a goal that the best data or build or design shop you know wouldn't find it a stretch of capacity to write a proposal in response to the RFP. Making allies of contract departments and contracting officers is helpful here.[4]

If you are connected with private-sector product companies, you can potentially help them satisfy the requirements that would enable government employees to license their software. Once they have done it once, they may be able to offer a standard government license and purchasing plan, which will make their products available to more people working in the field. There has been some work on the small services vendor side; for example, USDS and the Small Business Administration collaborated on a special contracting template for 8(a) companies[5] to offer digital-service builds or consulting.

---

3 SmartProcure and CoProcure are start-ups helping municipal procurement officials collaborate for better purchases.

4 Though often difficult, because they don't want to be biased by program staff or outsiders, so they're careful.

5 8(a) is a program of the Small Business Administration that limits competition for certain government contracts to small companies owned by disadvantaged Americans (https://www.sba.gov/federal-contracting/contracting-assistance-programs/8a-business-development-program).

LEGACY MIGRATIONS

If you spend any time around government software, you'll realize that some of the back-ends in particular are really, really old. This isn't a bad thing in itself! We should all aspire to have our production software provide decades of service with incremental updates. But there are many systems where those updates haven't been done, or haven't kept pace with current expectations about how software works and how institutions respond in service situations.

If you find yourself dealing with a system that (for example):

- has hours when the website is open and closed (probably because it uses overnight batch updates instead of writing new data as it's entered), and/or
- was built with an architecture where the community of vendors and experts is dwindling and not likely to be revived (like COBOL or some proprietary CMSs)

then yes, you have some version of a legacy system problem. If you can get permission and partnership to work on it, migrating that system to a more modern stack may be one of the best things you can do.

It is also one of the most challenging categories of project.

If you take on a legacy system problem, you are likely to encounter every other issue in this chapter in microcosm. It's really important to consider the time available, the capacity of the agency for major change, and the risk level. In most cases, a fundamental question will be whether it's best to go through a total rehauling and make one major cutover, or to move small pieces incrementally.

"Big Bang" migrations that attempt to rebuild everything and then do a hard cutover all at once are common in the annals of major procurements and software projects that have failed. An emerging best (but best of hard options) practice known as the "strangler" pattern[6] offers a

---

6 The strangler pattern is named for the strangler fig plant, not any nefarious human activities.

different approach to migration. Strangler patterns move small pieces, and move production traffic, until slowly the whole body of the old system is replaced. They require patience and cooperative partners and vendors, but there are some indications that the template can work in quite a few situations, as long as it's practiced with finesse[7].

Above all, legacy migration projects require strong partnerships and substantial resources. In the same way product management needs to balance tradeoffs in delivering new applications, that discipline is essential to sequencing and coordinating the components of a legacy project.

METRICS AND ANALYTICS

Over the past ten years, private-sector companies have leaned hard into quantitative metrics and practices tuned to work with them. Government practices, from web analytics through core service metrics, can seem underdeveloped by comparison. This is definitely an opportunity; helping decision-makers see that they need to (and can) test their assumptions is key. And creating space for the better use of data in decision-making is right in line with approaches like evidence-based policymaking that will be familiar within government. But it's not easy to directly translate tools and approaches built for the current private sector, especially for the web.

Nearly everything written about website management in recent years assumes that websites have one of two models: a conversion funnel or an ad-supported media model. All current products for measuring websites assume these as your goal. This framing results in other assumptions about what success looks like for a website:

- assuming you can draw valid inferences from, say, the most heavily trafficked pages on a site—which may

---

7 Dan Hon, who has worked on multiple government legacy migrations, pointed out a downside to me: the method's very tidiness can obscure the hard work that still needs to be done to existing systems.

not be true if the SEO is poor, there are variations in terminology, or the information architecture is not tidy
- assuming you want something from your user, which is only sometimes true in government[8]

All of this can be overcome with a thoughtful approach, but it's important not to assume that out-of-the box measurement tools, or simply counting what can be counted, will get you what you need.

If you are used to metrics primarily from web or app analytics, you may also find that it's harder to capture the data that answers your questions from back-end systems. The contract to initially set up a legacy system may or may not have covered data collection—and even if it did, the priorities may have since changed. It isn't always easy to collect an extra field or pivot how such systems record things, so creativity will be required. If you can't collect direct data on the questions you're interested in, just be mindful of hanging too much weight on proxy metrics.

Another common management-pleasing project is to create a dashboard for a department. It seems great, but it's hard to design dashboards to make clear how reliable each data component is. Instead, they tend to confer an equally authoritative appearance on everything on the screen. Don't fall into this trap if you're working with data. You'll do a huge service to your partners if you articulate the pitfalls of numerical metrics and how to check them against qualitative evidence like user research and open-ended constituent comments.

USER-CENTERED DESIGN

Some of the most magical changes I have ever seen as a civic technologist have come from making it possible for public servants who felt disconnected from their constituents to observe user

---

8 In the court system, for example, impartiality is one of the most foundational values—it needs to be easy for someone to start a legal proceeding, but the court can have no opinion about whether they should do it. So using a metric about increasing clicks or engagement might not be appropriate.

research and see the impact their work has for the people they serve. This powerful and accessible practice is one of the easiest for ordinary career government staff to adopt on their own, and it empowers them to be advocates for research and design.

There's no question that design is an essential discipline. Pretty much the only way to ensure that software, however well built, is actually useful for its intended purpose is to design it for (and ideally with) the people who will use it. As of 2020, design—with UX design as the leading component— is represented in every major digital service team at the federal, state, and municipal level.

Design disciplines from content strategy to wireframing and quick prototyping are most effective when they become part of the practice of the government entity, rather than something outsourced. I was recently delighted to meet the UX practice lead for the city of Philadelphia—the existence of a permanent and industry-legible position like this shows that design is now a valued and reasonably well-understood discipline in Philly.

But design does have its limits. User research observation may have a visceral effect on people who directly witness it, but report-outs of almost any kind will naturally dilute the impact, and have variable results in convincing anyone to change requirements or change software.

Public servants are used to responding to public feedback, but the channels and formats they typically use are very different. One common example is when a member of the public calls out an elected official at a public comment session, and the official responds by directing their staff to fix something without further research. Pausing such flurries in a hierarchical organization to allow for a proper assessment and appro- priate design is not always easy. That means the sooner researchers are able to establish a structured practice, the better, so as to have the tools and methods available when they're needed.

Like product managers, designers in government spend much of their time coaching, modeling, and teaching. Most design will move more slowly than would be the case in private-industry tech, partly because the practice of collaborative critique is something that many government staff are new to. Very many government staffers make what we would think of as design decisions on a daily basis—and many make good ones!—but critique is closely bound up in authority structures, and asking high-ranking people to explain their critiques is sometimes considered audacious. Overturning a high-ranking person's opinion with user feedback, even more so.

This is a cultural change worth modeling if you find yourself in a design role—it's the only way to show how to work intentionally with the powerful tool of design. The trick is to constantly work from a perspective of opening your practice and making the work accessible. It's frustrating that it's so unfamiliar, but if you accept that that's where you're starting, you can make space to coach and practice at the same time.

BRINGING CAPABILITIES INSIDE

For some efforts, your biggest indicator of impact may be the creation of permanent positions or groups staffed with people who know modern technology, which represents a sustainable commitment to using tech in a different way. Helping government change its hiring mix to include more skill sets from the technology range is one of the most durable ways to institute the changes civic tech wants to see—not just what would fit in an IT department, but product management, design, content strategy, data science, and so forth.

There is a whole area of civic tech work, usually referred to as "talent," that is about adjusting government job descriptions, serving as a bridge between existing job classes and necessary skill sets, and matching skilled people with hiring managers who need them. This involves creativity and flexibility on everyone's part, but it can result in some of the most lasting impacts for a civic tech project of any size or length.

Here's a look at how we might map traditional private-sector tech roles onto in-house government roles:

- Engineering, at least in some of its subdisciplines, is probably the most legible tech skill area for governments; there are application developer job descriptions that are close enough for private-sector engineers to recognize.
- Design would be next; there are job descriptions that can be repurposed so that a particular business analyst position is known to be customarily a UX position. However, that kind of informal change is brittle. Something more major is afoot if the title is changed to say "UX" instead. Other design disciplines map less clearly.
- Product management is almost entirely new, and most often starts out being done by consultants or civic tech term staff; expanding it beyond that group is a major win.

But keep in mind that civic tech is a *hybrid* field; you aren't stuck with just these private-sector tech disciplines in their pure form. One of the most exciting changes we've seen in my current consulting work with the California Courts is the creation of a permanent Web Content Attorney position. Since no content for the courts is authoritative unless it's written by an attorney, but no content works for non-attorney users unless it's carefully written to plain-language web-writing standards, this position is a bridge and requires a person who combines both skill sets. If we achieved nothing else (don't worry, we've done more), that would be a long-term impact on that organization for the public good.

Don't miss opportunities to train or coach career staff, and especially don't miss opportunities to embed a modern technology practice within the personnel structure of your partner organization, either by advocating for new roles or updating the descriptions of existing ones. We've learned more and more that civic tech jobs are change jobs as well as technical jobs, and this is one of the ways to make change work last.

MOVING TRADITIONAL ENTITIES FORWARD

There's a special category of project for people who want to bring either a government entity or a part of the traditional ecosystem into line with

the values and practices of civic tech. Such projects are probably better suited for experienced civic technologists rather than first-timers.

Maybe your city, county, or state government doesn't have an innovation lab or digital service team yet. Getting one started is a huge service—and a major, long-term effort. You'll need to be very familiar with the achievements, budgets, and pitfalls of the existing teams.[9] You should also expect a considerable amount of relationship- and trust-building with stakeholders to precede action. You may be able to do this through a volunteer group, or by figuring out who can support your pitch to the relevant executives. This entails learning about both the executives and their priorities. You might meet such people at a hackathon, but one hackathon, even if you spend a lot of time with them and even if your project wins, probably isn't enough. Expect this to take time and (metaphorical) sweat.

This is another useful way of thinking about projects to change how governments hire and manage their technology teams and how they procure technology services. Both of these areas are heavily regulated, but enormous foundational change is possible for people with legal and policy skills who build strong relationships. Work like this can help to:

- identify structures for digital teams,
- adjust job classes and budgets to enable hiring people from modern tech disciplines, and
- interpret or change purchasing rules to enable governments to attract and contract with high-capacity modern vendors.

Any of these has the potential to transform an agency for the better, and it's extremely valuable work that supports every other branch of the civic tech field.

If you want to improve the tech options available to governments, but you don't want to be part of a start-up, one more possibility is to join a not-very-digital, traditional government vendor and help them become

---

9 Most of the existing digital teams maintain public blogs and GitHub repos; "work in the open" is a durable principle that has persisted across oceans and quite a few years.

more capable in the digital arena. This may not be the most glamorous assignment in the civic tech space, but it's potentially a very impactful one if you can pull it off. Don't try to pull a stealth move—definitely pitch yourself as someone who can help the vendor both win and satisfy modern digital contracts. (You will likely need the credibility of having worked inside a government agency to do this successfully.) Highlight your knowledge of both sides of the space and your past successes with digital transformation. This kind of capacity-building is needed across the ecosystem, which is enormous.

• • •

The methods we've covered in this chapter are advanced, and will call on you to use every ounce of your status as a technologist—the very same status that I advise using with awareness of privilege (Chapter 2) and a restrained relationship with innovation (Chapter 5). Civic tech efforts that sweep in with forced changes can be brittle; long-term success requires a subtler strategy. Genuine solidarity with the ongoing efforts and struggles of public servants is key to success in meeting urgent public needs amid heavy constraints. Act so your partners recognize you as someone on their side, working to solve problems together.

Solidarity with the public mission means you're amplifying the needs of the public servants who are working in the same space, understanding and to some degree accommodating the pressures that exist in their working environment. When you see such people—and they are absolutely everywhere—take it as your mission to make their good work easier and give it greater reach. Combine this with one or two of the other methods and you will have enormous potential for real change.

CHAPTER 11

HARMONIZING WAYS OF WORKING

A worthwhile goal of civic technology is to mutually infuse an understanding of technology and government goals, and to establish methods of working collaboratively towards those shared aims. Working as closely together as possible is the only way to go about it. Respecting each other as capable creatures from alien worlds—tech world and government world, separated by light years—won't do the trick. Figuring out how to share the same world is where it's at.

We're all human, and it's all too easy to get caught up in group divisions. Tech-oriented teams in particular have a tendency to come across as people with unattainable specialized knowledge and mysterious processes that are beyond ordinary people's ability to access. If we don't push back against this with intentional openness and inclusivity, everything we achieve will be short-lived. We'll also miss the chance to become more humble and collaborative versions of ourselves.

WORK CULTURE: TECH VERSUS GOVERNMENT

Many tech workers have spent most or all of their career in an environment where real-time collaboration is the default way of working. The advent of ubiquitous Wi-Fi, laptops, and truly shared editing has enabled a style of collaboration in the modern tech office that is qualitatively different from what came before. This style has only been possible in the past decade; most governments don't yet have the infrastructural building blocks of real-time collaboration in 2020 (though the COVID-19 crisis is forcing many forward), so teams work in an older style. With care, these two styles can work together, but it's worth looking at the differences to understand how to create a bridge between them.

In a modern tech work environment, cloud-based shared documents and repositories are the norm, and it's possible to work together closely from different locations. People collaborate directly through comments and suggested changes (and pull requests, if they're engineers), which means feedback cycles can be very short. Email may be less relied on as a communication channel if people can talk about work products in ways that are attached to the work products themselves.

Before 2010 or so, it was a lot harder, though not impossible, to collaborate on a document in real time, so people mostly didn't. One person would draft a document and email it out for comment, and then after receiving a round of feedback, send out another draft.[1] Rinse and repeat. This mostly asynchronous setup is still the predominant one in government work spaces.

The result of these differences is that for a person used to the practices of the private-sector tech industry, collaboration in government spaces will appear slow and surprisingly involved in hierarchy and sign-offs. Someone watching the current tech style from a classic government environment may find it both opaque and irresponsibly fast, without clear decision points or lines of authority.

---

1 Microsoft Word's Track Changes feature was essential in enabling this style of revision and collaboration. Despite being the butt of many jokes, it was a critical affordance for collaborative document work before the advent of online shared docs.

The relative availability of modern computer equipment can also be a point of some division between tech and government office cultures. Many government work spaces are modernizing their conference rooms and offering Wi-Fi throughout their buildings, but laptops are tougher—they are expensive to replace regularly and the public doesn't fund government agencies at a level where all of them can afford it. A seemingly neutral act like equipping a digital team with MacBooks can have the effect of creating a bubble of tech culture around it, and may even breed resentment from other teams accustomed to years of scrimping under a scarcity mentality.

Bridging this gap requires some self-awareness. If your group has some specialized tools, walls featuring a bunch of sticky notes, a metrics dashboard on a screen, and a drawerful of snacks, I'm not worried. Those things can all be used to invite people in. But if you also have much nicer computers, later daily start times, and a separate dress code from your partners, you might be in danger of creating a bubble. This risks alienating any existing group that had previously been thought of as the innovators; furthermore, it insulates its beneficiaries from the real working conditions of their colleagues. If they're out of touch with this reality, they aren't likely to design and build things that will truly work in the government environment for the long term.

People in government often work in the same organization, and with the same colleagues, for a decade or more—sometimes multiple decades. Interpersonal conflict can unfortunately play out over the very long term. You may feel inclined to dismiss this as pettiness, but far better is to acknowledge the genuine feelings of frustration, and direct your focus to what these teams have achieved in spite of considerable constraints. What they may lack in terms of speedy adaptability they often make up for with instructive workarounds and years of valuable institutional knowledge. Combining that hard-earned wisdom with technological creativity is a recipe for real progress in civic tech.

YOUR JARGON, MY JARGON

Every work culture has its own special language, and when separate cultures meet one another, it's common to think of other people's special language as "jargon." Misunderstandings and minor disagreements over the use of language are endemic to workspaces where people from different backgrounds and disciplines collaborate. These inevitable moments can be healthy and productive as long as everyone starts from the assumption that their language is simply one among many, and mostly[2] no better than any other.

Take a moment to think about any jargon you might use. Have you recently asked someone to, for example, slack you the VC link for the retro? Or could you see yourself asking that? Could you understand such a request? It's 100 percent incomprehensible to someone without the contextual knowledge required to understand that *Slack* is a messaging app's name being used as a verb, *VC* can mean "venture capitalist" but in reference to meetings means "videoconference," and *retro* is short for "retrospective," a special meeting format that is part of Agile-derived working culture. Using this language doesn't make you bad, but placing any judgment on the knowledge needed to understand it can make it much harder to collaborate. If someone told you about the BCP they're working on for 23–24 based on the CJ's Futures Report, you might feel equally at sea.[3]

Questions can also come up when the same word has different connotations for different groups. One of my worst language misunderstandings happened at Code for America when we were pitching a project to a municipal partner as "lightweight." We meant lightweight as in lean, without extra maintenance headaches, and sustainable; our partners heard lightweight as in not robust, not serious, not ready for prime time. It took a couple of weeks for us to figure out how we were all missing one another's points.

---

2 Work languages centered on particular issues can have more thoughtful or complete language-structures for working with those issues.

3 That'd be the Budget Change Proposal for the 2023–24 legislative budget cycle, based on the Chief Justice's Futures Report.

If you're collaborating with partners who work on fisheries management, you'll need to learn some of their precise working language related to populations, measurement types, and permitting. And if you're introducing a new practice like sprints, you'll need to teach some of that vocabulary to your partners. Both of you may be puzzled at times by language used by the procurement group. But predictable hiccups in communication can be fixed with more up-front communication.

Setting a team norm that asking questions about unfamiliar vocabulary and usages is welcome from everyone is a good start. Creating a collaborative team glossary that everyone can contribute to can take it further. But the most important thing is an open attitude to partners' usages and a lightly held attachment to your own.

TECHNIQUES OF PROFESSIONAL INCLUSION

It's likely you'll need to exercise your powers of influence in an unfamiliar or uncomfortable productivity technology landscape. If you have made a career of adapting to different tech stacks and environments, it's so very worth deploying that adaptability to meet your partners where they are: it will make the working environment more inclusive for everyone as it evolves to accommodate new technological methods.

If you're used to Slack, Google Docs, and video calls, you may need to remap your communication patterns to email, MS Word Track Changes, and conference calls. You may find yourself working with people who use email more formally with the conventions of letters, and (if they have a military background) sign their emails with v/r (very respectfully) instead of a breezy or cute salutation.

The techniques of professional inclusion are simple (though not always easy) and most of them come down to communication work and—especially—meetings (regardless of what current tech culture may say about meetings being bad in general). Here are just a few of the ways I've deployed these techniques in my time in civic tech:

- holding office hours for people who need to make design decisions

- bringing in speakers for lunch-and-learns about technology topics
- joining governance and advisory boards for projects
- starting clubs for learning new techniques like web writing and CSS
- sending weekly email newsletters to a broad set of project stakeholders
- teaching partners who are new to GitHub to contribute (even just text!) and submit pull requests
- inviting partners along on user research sessions

Think about how you might be able to use similar techniques to open your practice to curious people in your immediate team and beyond.

RIGIDITY AND HIERARCHY

One of the biggest things to be mindful of is whether you're helping your partners gain the skills to work in a flexible and collaborative way or, instead, installing another rigid process.

Rigidity in government is partly an effect of the technological discrepancies we've already discussed, but it's also due to the more hierarchical and separated structure of government teams. Multidisciplinary build teams are a rare structure in government. Program staff traditionally stay out of IT matters, and IT staff stay out of program matters. They do work together—on a fairly typical project, a CIO[4] shop would engage a vendor to build something a program group wants—but not closely, and not with a lot of give and take.

In the above example, the vendor staff probably wouldn't colocate with either of the other groups. The process would be formal and would flow according to requirements documents, change requests, and acceptance tests. Civic technologists have to be very explicit about the different processes we expect. Too many times, I've seen a civic tech crew offer a prototype hoping for feedback, only to have an inside group accept it

---

4 Chief Information Officer, a common title for the head of an IT department. By contrast, Chief Technical Officer (CTO) positions are rare in government.

as-is and start creating workarounds shared only among themselves. This happens when teams work from an assumption that things can't be changed once handed off, and that critiquing people who have management support can be dangerous. In this situation, the civic tech team needs to overcommunicate how easy changes are (a live update as a demo can sometimes do the trick) and how welcome and needed honest critique is.

In organizations that are used to rigid processes (and to penalties for not following them), it's very easy to just adopt the next process and bolt on the same penalties and fears. Process may be driven by lower-status workers who create submissions or requests that are then reviewed or approved by people with higher status. In this situation, showing work to a reviewer is scary; the work needs to be as thought-out as it can be before the reviewer sees it. Reviewers in these dynamics may not see it as a true collaboration; they may just say yes, or no, or try again, instead of offering feedback.

The incentives could not be more different from an environment where peers show each other early drafts and are excited to discover mistakes early. More modern rituals and tools can support this collaborative way of working, but they won't create the shift on their own. You'll need to model and demonstrate everything—from sharing crummy early work to being excited about discovering where you're wrong to including members of different disciplines in working groups that persist over time. It's culture-change work, and it can be hard and slow.

• • •

If your past few years of work have taken place in a real-time collaboration environment where teamwork is supported by low hierarchy and worker empowerment, you may be genuinely thrown when trying to collaborate in an environment that doesn't have real-time affordances, or that is transitioning to them with a lot of discomfort. For me, the shift that matters is the one toward open and real-time (or quickly episodic) collaboration among people at different levels and from different disciplines. I recognize how much productivity tools do to enable that, but I don't believe they are its foundation.

If you can model effective cross-disciplinary collaboration using the tools in place, and invite more and more people to participate, then you can create this shift even before you're able to switch up the toolsets. This requires the humility to use tools that may not be your preference, and to level up your communications, but it's some of the most valuable and lasting work you can do if you have the privilege of working within government.

CHAPTER 12

THE ALLIES WE NEED

Nearly all civic tech projects will need support and partnership from civic entities to succeed in the long term. This means a significant part of the work for practitioners is to actively seek partners and allies, and invest in being strong partners and allies themselves. Project leaders and seniors will often take the initiative in partnerships, but every team member has a role to play in keeping those partnerships strong.

It's *possible* to start certain kinds of civic tech projects from an essentially adversarial perspective. Critiquing a government system or interface has, a few times, led to an invitation to improve it.[1] But even if you choose a strategy of critique at some stage of your project, it's a very good idea to do it in a way that won't preclude the possibility of a partnership later. That means respectful language, no speculation about ulterior motives or intellectual capacity, and a critique clearly anchored to a key value like public service or stewardship. Carefully done, this can

---

1 For example, Code for America's GetCalFresh project started as a "guerrilla" alternate interface intended to show the gaps in existing business process.

sometimes open doors, which is the real goal. In most cases, though, approaching the agency as a friend is best.

In this chapter, I examine different categories of allies, how they're helpful to civic tech projects, and what it takes to secure and maintain relationships with them. I also go into types of allies that bring risks with them and how to consider how close you want to get.

EXECUTIVE CHAMPIONS AND STRATEGIC ALIGNMENT

Most people will think quickly of executive support as a critical category of alliance. For me, though, executive support falls in the "necessary but not sufficient" space. It's very hard to make progress without executive support, or at least executive tolerance, but in pursuing high-level endorsement, it's important to note the political nature of government leadership.

Plan to factor the political status of your executives into your thinking. If an election the administration isn't certain to win is coming up, you do not want to be closely associated with elected leadership. It's much better in this circumstance to pursue a quieter style of support in the more administrative leadership ranks, because when—not *if*—a new administration is elected, many heads of departments will be replaced with new appointments. Pet initiatives of the previous administration may no longer be favored, either. (This is part of why it can be hard to start new things close to an election.)

If you have several years' runway before an election, or if the administration is looking strong for reelection, it may make sense to pursue top-level executive endorsement. Getting an elected or appointed leader to make your goals a priority can give them a major boost and, with enough time, you may be able to show results that make your program hard to cancel in the future.

With all that calculation in mind, what does it take to win the confidence and support of agency leaders? Be aware that you'll definitely have to deal with people who don't think of themselves as tech people; even quite a few federal government CIOs are people from a legal or policy, rather than tech, background.

Executive alignment becomes easier when you can pitch your work in terms that people who aren't passionate about technology for its own sake can understand. These leaders are looking for how your technology proposals align with policy goals and strategy. You'll need to align your product, design, and technical goals with the language of mission achievement, efficiency, and risk management. You may also need to create a more explicit, step-by-step plan than you would do in a pure Agile or Lean environment. If you think of the plan as a continuous translation of your working documents, rather than a precursor that blocks you from starting, you can still move quickly.

Don't think of this as compromising your principles—it's meeting very important stakeholders where they are. You may also need to present proposals and plans in a more formal format than you would in a tech company, so be prepared to spend some time on the project of winning the executive support you need. It can also be a win to seem different, new, and innovative—many executives are excited by newness—but simple things like higher-quality graphics and charts will often achieve this.

MID-LEVEL, SOCIALLY CONNECTED PARTNERS

Getting support (or at least forbearance) from the top will ease your path, but it's not sufficient. When we researched digital transformation at 18F in 2016, we discovered that a key factor in the sustainment of innovation initiatives was the active support of well-connected, mid-tenured career staff.

These are people who have been at an agency for maybe ten or fifteen years and hold ranks like program manager, senior analyst, or manager. They are uniquely positioned to project credibility to everyone in the organization, both "up" and "down" the hierarchy, and they have a wealth of information about history. Frontline staff feel comfortable sharing concerns with them, and executives check in with them to see how new ideas will play or find out what the staff really think. Those who combine this position with strong social skills and interest can often be found serving on committees, taking "detail" assignments where they temporarily embed with another department or agency, and generally making friends. If you can get one or two people of this sort as active partners, everything becomes possible.

How to find them? For one thing, the person you're looking for is likely curious and engaged and may ask about your work even if they're not immediately involved. They're very likely running some kind of governance board, webmasters' learning collective, or domain-specific book club—possibly several at once. I realized I'd met one of these people while I was working on a particularly tough bureaucratic tangle at GSA. My partner and I had been fairly well stuck, but one day people began to show up at our door saying that Angela[2] had told them we should meet. Angela had attended an earlier meeting where we'd introduced our project, which initially won us none of the clarity we'd been hoping for. But it turned out that Angela knew everyone, and after she had put the word out that our project was worthwhile, contacts suddenly became easier to find and things began to move.

If you're very lucky, such a person will have already raised their hand to work on something new, and you'll meet them at your kickoff. If it's not clear from there, asking "Who can introduce me to people all over the [department/agency/bureau/city]?" should start to get you some ideas.

When you find this person, greet them as a potential ally and find out how you can help them, while telling them about your project. Absolutely agree to present to the lunch-and-learn group or the governance board. Make your team available for any meetings they think you need to have, and listen to everything they say about how things *really* work around here.

In contrast to higher-level staff, this person is going to stay in place when a new administration comes in, and they'll have a surprising amount

---

2 Angela is a real name, though I won't share her last name. If the Angela who unstuck my project ever reads this, I want her to know I still think about that help with gratitude.

of power over how quickly and from what angle the new administration's changes get implemented. Small shifts in practice supported by committed public servants in these ranks can have huge effects.

LEGAL AND REGULATORY COLLEAGUES

Colleagues from the compliance or legal department are the kind of allies you can expect to ask you hard questions, keep you honest, and explain the *why* behind how things currently work. If you can create a relationship based on transparency and trust, you will be in a position to remove many obstacles from the path of your work. Seek their advice early, and ignore them at your peril.

Compliance team colleagues can be underrated allies to multi-disciplinary teams and iterative development in general, and the earlier you involve them in your project, the better. Ask them for their input at a sketch level: "We're thinking of putting part of this process online, in public. Can you see any regulations we should be aware of? Are there any risks we should be tracking?" Attend to their feedback and keep asking them what they think about each new version as you move toward a prototype and eventually a launch.

You don't want them to be in the position of being the final reviewer looking at a nearly finished project for the first time and having to nix it—and honestly, they don't want to be that person, either. If you make them part of the process at each step, you can get their input at higher and higher levels of detail and fidelity. The final prelaunch stage will not be a surprise, and their questions about it likely won't be a surprise, either (in fact, they should have been answered at one of the intermediate stages).

Having the support of the legal or compliance folks can also put you in a position to counter one of the most common objections from people who are just nervous about new things: "I'm intrigued, but has legal seen this?" With their support in place, you can confidently answer, "Yes, Carla has been involved from the beginning; she's such a great partner, I can send you her latest review." Suddenly what might have delayed your project for months becomes a very different conversation.

Above all, don't wait to approach your legal department or compliance officer—find out whom to talk to there, and set up an early meeting to establish a relationship and understand their needs.

PARTNERS FROM OUTSIDE GOVERNMENT

Government is only one part of the civic ecosystem, and whether you plan to work on the inside or outside of government for your project, it's well worth having conversations with involved advocates. Nongovernmental organizations (NGOs) are deeply involved in delivering services in areas like legal help, food aid, and medical care, and are also important partners in collecting data on programs and advocating for improvements.

Some advocacy organizations explicitly call for policy change via legislation or otherwise, and some work within current rules to deliver services to the public. They may know of pitfalls in the policy you plan for your software to express, or they may be able to add their support with government officials with whom they have a relationship. But before they do that, they'll need to see that you and your project are worth using time or political capital on. Be ready to show them.

Here are some key outside allies your project might include:

- Staff of NGOs that supplement government services in your area will have plenty of opinions about what their clients need and how well your agency is serving them. Whether they have a friendly or adversarial relationship with your agency, it's worth seeking them out for conversation—but take care to give advance notice to internal stakeholders in the latter case.
- Community groups can share all kinds of historical context and help you reach out to people you hope to do research with and ultimately to serve.

- Public librarians encounter questions about almost every civic subject under the sun and help people find resources. They also have access to clean, ADA-compliant spaces where you may be able to do user research with permission.

For a more specific example, let's look at the landscape for legal work. In most US court systems, each court has judicial and administrative independence, but there is a central rule-setting body.[3] The courts receive budget allocations from the legislature, but they also charge fees for filings and a few other things; the judiciary is formally a separate and independent branch of government. Partnerships with court staff and officers are obviously critical.

But there are further players in the legal arena, and if you're working with the court system, it's helpful to have connections to people working in these adjacent areas:

- legal aid organizations, independent nonprofits that offer direct legal services and advocate for policy
- the state Bar Association, which licenses attorneys, advocates for policy, and can also offer referrals to pro bono attorneys
- law libraries, which provide research resources for lawyers and the public; these are independent nonprofits established by law, but usually have close ties to their local court
- nonprofit organizations that help people with particular legal issues like evictions, domestic violence, or debt lawsuits
- groups that focus on more general "access to justice," often including digital means to pursue legal matters

Any group within an analogous list for your topic area would be a valuable ally, depending on your specific project and strategy. Connecting with them might involve attending a conference, paying a visit, or writing a pitch, any of which could put you in a position to learn a great deal and support people who are already doing the work.

---

3 This will be called something like the Administrative Office of the Courts or Judicial Council, depending on the state.

In all of these cases, think about your ethical and reciprocal obligations. If you're not a member of the community, some groups in any of these categories may be skeptical of you and your work at first. You need to demonstrate that you're a trustworthy partner who will take care of their needs all the way through your process. Here are some simple things you can do to show this:

- Start early and expect multiple meetings. Offer to go to the groups, wherever they work, instead of expecting them to come to you.
- Be completely transparent about your process—if you want to do user research, for example, share your full script and your data plans in advance. Then, afterward, share your aggregated data and exactly what you learned. (Even better if you invite these stakeholders to participate in synthesis with you.)
- Be clear about whether you're building a prototype and what that means. Don't make promises you or your partners can't back up.
- Offer to share information and tech skills with members of the group. Show them your GitHub repos if you have them, and help anyone who is interested to join and try out contributing.
- Use your best manners. (I'm not kidding. Gratitude and kindness matter enormously.)

COMMUNICATIONS AND THE PRESS

One of the pillars of a free society is a free press that investigates power and tells the truth. Reporters write about government all the time, sometimes from a political perspective (who's winning what, what the arguments are) and other times from a more critical angle—perhaps on the use of public money, or whether service delivery is working well. Reporters can expose problems that we civic technologists believe we can solve, and they can also expose our own mistakes. All of this is good.

Many technologists are used to sharing stories (or having their company PR departments do it) with the trade press, which often goes easier on stars in its own industry. The technology press has broken many important scandals, but also uncritically reports press releases from tech giants. Local news also has something of a booster function for local civic institutions in addition to its investigative responsibilities. But it's important to note that many government staff won't be as familiar with this experience; they're more likely to encounter the press in its oversight role, and sometimes feel that it's unfair.

The press can be an ally in highlighting the problems you're trying to solve, or informing the public about new services available. Getting the press to highlight problems is an important technique for advocacy, but actively doing so as a civic technologist can sometimes make other government allies mistrustful. It fits in the category of adversarial approaches that should be used with care. (If you are ever featured in a scandalous story for breaking a rule you didn't know existed, you may be able to sympathize.)

If you're working within a government office, establishing good relationships with the reporters who cover your agency is a good practice, and you'll need a close connection with your press office or public information officer to do it. You want public affairs to feel comfortable referring questions about your area to you, or putting forward a story about your work. Under no circumstances should you work around such a department if you have one.

It's also useful to collaborate with your public affairs shop to prepare for likely press attention on the occasion of launches, upgrades, or even outages. Bullet points or even a full press release about what problem your team's work solves, and how it makes things better for constituents or more efficient for the institution, are good assets to have on hand. This is also a great place to highlight the leadership and roles of the career staff work you work with; the press sometimes underreports on the long, hard work of getting funding and support for the beautiful tech things you built, and it's good allyship on your part to celebrate the shared success with everyone involved. Any storytelling you do for public purposes will benefit other civic tech teams as well.

• • •

There's a saying that if you want to go fast, go alone, but if you want to go far, go together. Civic tech is a strong use case for this—a small, isolated group can build a valuable prototype quickly, and satisfy that first step of showing what's possible. But when you want to create lasting change, part of doing what's necessary is to seek all the alliances you can get. Respect, transparency, and helpfulness will always go a long way toward building those. And whatever your technical discipline, you should consider forging alliances part of your work and plan to spend ample time and energy on it.

CHAPTER 13

PACE, RISKS, AND SELF-CARE

If there's one thing I hope you've taken away from the earlier chapters, it's that this work is hard. Compelling, rewarding, full of wonderful colleagues, and really very hard. I like to think of it as a collaborative fifty-year project to enable our government to use technology as a tool to better serve the public. Fifty years is a long time. Whatever project you take on, you'll be carrying some of the weight of that time line and that goal.

Nearly all civic technologists need to do change work as well as their technical specialty, and doing change work well is taxing, period. The day-to-day work has all of the usual stress of deadlines, team interactions, problem solving, and trade-offs, and often with a more complicated organizational landscape to navigate than is typical in the private sector.

Long-term victories in civic tech often come with a lot of short-term losses along the way. No matter your track record, you *will* lose battles, and you will have projects fail. Not just occasional failures, either—failures or partial successes are pretty likely outcomes. Losing is tiring; if you're able to draw lessons out of those failures and share them with the community, they won't be in vain, but that too demands something of your personal resources.

It's worth thinking about risks you need to prepare for with this work, and making a plan for pacing and personal sustainability. Whether you're reading this before your first civic tech project or fifteen years in, I offer this chapter as a call to reflect on your resources and how you can sustain your capacities.

ROTATIONS, TERMS, AND THE LONG TERM

If you sign up for a rescue effort, or a fellowship, or even a political campaign, you know that your project has an end date (though in the case of a rescue effort, you might not know exactly when). You can decide how hard to push for that amount of time, but you should anticipate that the work may be more taxing than you're used to. People who worked on the HealthCare.gov rescue in 2013 worked fifteen-hour days for months; many of them experienced physical and mental health effects. Be aware that if you accept these kinds of hours, you will need extra support and care. Figure out how you can get it. If you haven't previously worked with a therapist or coach, this may be a time when you want to. If you deal with physical conditions or mental-health issues that are exacerbated by stress, it's worth having a plan in place in advance.

By contrast, some government jobs build in a fail-safe of sorts that protects anyone from fifteen-hour days by restricting workweeks to forty hours—no more, no less—from the administrative level. This can cause its own kind of stress by making variable workloads difficult to manage; workers don't have the option to balance a fifty-five-hour week when a release is imminent with a twenty-five-hour week when a bunch of things are blocked. But it can be wise to stick to a forty-hour rhythm, especially if your partners do the same.

Contract jobs through vendors or directly with governments are usually not subject to the exact same restrictions, although in some cases there may be restrictions on when hours can be billed. I sometimes end up working hours I can't bill when we have a short-term mission goal that's really critical. I'll tell you *pro forma* that you should never do this; it doesn't serve the long-term goals of civic tech for governments to see an underestimated view of how much labor good digital work takes. Remember that the goal is not just for your current project to succeed, but for your partners to be able to sustain and evaluate good modern tech work into the future. Once in a while isn't a huge deal, but if you find yourself regularly working non-billable hours, you absolutely must reevaluate.

With long-term work, you need to work at a pace you can sustain for years, accounting for the level of effort. There are quite a few ways to arrange this, depending on other aspects of your personal situation. One way is to take significant amounts of time off between rounds of term work.[1] The more "off" your time off can be, the better. Another is to hew strictly to government customs around forty-hour workweeks: don't answer or look at work email during off hours or weekends, and cultivate really salient activities, whether it's family life, athletics, or formal hobbies, when you're not at work.

You will almost certainly be tempted to overcommit if you're excited about the mission; I see you and I salute you. I absolutely end up there myself, but I've been at this long enough to know that I need to take care.

PACING YOURSELF

After the COVID lockdowns went into place in the spring of 2020, digital teams representing various government services worked overtime and on weekends to respond to immediate needs like getting informational websites up and shoring up online unemployment insurance apps. For these initial responses, this was the right call. As governments get their feet under them after this or any disaster, there will be much more to be done, but work should revert to nonemergency mode. Long-term policy

---

1 Given the vagaries of contracting, you may end up with no choice—if that's what you encounter, make the most of it.

changes stemming from the disaster (remote court rules, for example) will take time, and tech should also move with deliberation to support them. It's a shift in mindset for mission-focused techies to intentionally hew to a sustainable pace, but it's worth distinguishing the red-hot emergencies (like a new pandemic) from the "so many needs, not enough time" outlook I've seen burn out civic tech workers with the best of intentions.

The public's needs are urgent, no question, but you need to do a few calculations to make sure you remain able to serve them. Don't start impossible projects, for one. If you have the opportunity to do something enormous, look really hard at the project's resource level; even if it's good, break the work into smaller pieces so it's easier to manage mentally. Arrange space for your team to have achievable wins along the way, even if the overall issue remains daunting.

Some of the most compelling problems may not be solvable with the tools or support you're reasonably able to access; if you find yourself in such a situation, your best bet may be a strategic retreat. Tenacity is wonderful, but tenacity in an impossible endeavor leads to burnout, and we need you whole.

Think also about whether you're signing up for a 10k, a marathon, or an ultramarathon,[2] and plan your pacing, recharging, and care accordingly. There are now four-year renewable terms at some federal agencies, meaning you can stay eight years if you want to. A lot of life changes can happen in eight years—and in many places, an administration transition is a guarantee. That's a truly long term commitment.

For that length of time, doing work that taxes your professional and social capacities every day, you need the working conditions to be reasonably comfortable. Even something like a time-zone mismatch that has you on 7:00 a.m. calls multiple times a week can be unsustainable over four or five years, though it might be okay for four or five months. Your needs can be whatever they are for you, as long as you consider what will sap or sustain your personal resilience over the course of years.

---

2 There's really no such thing as a civic tech sprint engagement.

You can expect that the days and weeks will be hard, however long you stay, and that may mean it makes sense to adopt a fairly careful attitude toward things like travel or after-hours work if you're staying a long time.

THE LOGISTICS BURDEN

If you work for a nonprofit, you may be very used to the level of support provided in government offices (in fact, in contrast to people transitioning from tech, your first government job may offer a better salary and more perks).

If you've been an empowered worker at a well-funded start-up or a tech company that is competing for people, you may not realize the level of support you're accustomed to. It's worth taking stock, because even though it seems minor, these little things can and do add up.

Most people coming from a tech office manage their own computers, and the IT department will often authorize any kind of setup or SaaS product desired. Not so in government offices. If you're issued a government computer or phone, it's usually going to be fairly restricted in what you can install. It could also be heavily monitored, and so might any software services issued by the agency you're partnering with.

Importantly, if you do something like set up your government email on your personal phone for convenience, that might mean your personal phone would be subject to search in an investigation. Kind of an extreme circumstance, but if you've become accustomed to using one device for everything, you might want to reconsider.

So you may need another device for yourself, and you may need to deal with the hassle of switching between government and personal devices. (I'll point out, though, that this can be useful in disconnecting fully during your off times, which is a good idea.)

In tech companies' management culture, personal career advancement is important, to the extent that managers are often invested in it as a goal for their staff. You may be able to get paid to travel to conferences and meet others in your field. If these are your baseline, you may be disoriented by the (not wrong, just different) level of support provided to government employees. For example, training will likely be supported in a government job only if it develops a skill that directly benefits your current assignment—and even if it does, the budget will be low and strictly scrutinized. You'll be much more likely to receive support in the form of community college classes than of travel to conferences.

Then there are the really little details, like where you pick up your 2:00 p.m. coffee. Tech offices often have free, excellent coffee and tea; if things are good, you probably have a selection of snacks in the office, and if things are really good, free meals. It's something you don't have to think about. It's minor, but the companies do it because it frees their staff to focus on work.

The public does not generally pay for free food or beverages for those serving, not even office coffee; many departments organize coffee clubs where employees pay into a fund to make coffee easily available for contributors. Sometimes public budgets don't allow easy replacement of things like refrigerators or microwaves in office kitchens; I've seen people crowdsourcing funds to replace one, or going without.

To be clear, none of these things are a huge deal, and I don't expect you to find them a huge deal—but I do want you to think about the little bits of capacity they consume in thinking about what support systems you need to set up for yourself.

FINANCIAL RISKS AND PLANNING

Government jobs are a watchword for stability, but there are risks— some of which are specific to actual government jobs, and others that show up along with the patchwork of contracts, special hiring authorities, and fellowship work.

Although it's very hard to fire or lay off career government workers (that is, W-2 government employees), it is possible to furlough them, fully or partially. Several Bay Area municipal governments had long-term partial furloughs that reduced workers' income by 5 percent or 10 percent in the 2010s. While rare, the federal government can be shut down if Congress is deadlocked on a budget issue; if that happens, federal workers aren't paid for the duration (though historically, back pay has always been approved once the government reopens). At the end of 2018, the federal government was shut down for nearly five weeks over multiple episodes.

If you're on contract status, things can also change quickly. Vendors whose contracts are canceled or curtailed may shed staff quickly to stay afloat. Contracting itself may cause gaps in work or just in payment. As a contract worker in government, I've experienced gaps in work during renewal periods, just because the paperwork took longer than expected; I've experienced very long hiring timelines followed by urgent start dates. I've seen budget changes that caused surprise changes in contract end dates. Expect these problems, unfortunately; if you can afford to keep a few weeks' or months' worth of expenses in a savings account, it's a really good idea to do so.

If you're hired in a leadership role in a federal or state agency, you should carry professional liability insurance. As an expense, this runs around $200–400/year, protects your personal assets (your savings, house, etc.), and provides some coverage for legal fees if you are named in a lawsuit against your agency, or found at fault in an investigation.

You should also check your bank account more than you might otherwise—an interesting feature of government work is that accidental overpayments do happen, and will be considered debts to the government once discovered. It's in your interest to find any, identify how to pay them back, and follow instructions to the letter, documenting them fully. Your inside contacts should be able to help if this happens, but you should be aware of the risk and keep an eye out

HOW TO RECOGNIZE BURNOUT

There's tired and then there's burned out—and they form something of a spectrum. Tiredness can accumulate and turn into burnout over time.

But you need to be able to recognize the danger signs, and if you reach a state of true burnout, you're going to need a significant period (likely months) of complete time off. "Deep" time off can shorten the rest period some, if your situation allows you to do things like take a vacation with your phone turned off for several weeks. But for true burnout there is no remedy other than serious rest, and your long-term mental health will depend on taking that rest if you get to that point.

A while ago, I spoke with a civic tech colleague whose yearslong stretch on the same project had been especially taxing. He had an overwhelming sense of just *not wanting to*, in general. Furthermore, he had taken short vacations—the kind of time off that would have restored his mojo in the past—and had returned to work only to find the same *don't want to* waiting for him. This unshakable *don't want to* is the hallmark of burnout, and it may even escalate to *can't*, especially if work challenges are combined with other stresses. If you reach a stage where you cannot make yourself go to work that you generally enjoy, seek professional support right away.

Although burnout can be sneaky as it accumulates, it's best to take a preventive approach so you don't end up out of commission for months at a time. That means finding a way for yourself, and ideally someone else who knows you well, to keep an eye on your frustration and tiredness levels.

Bear in mind that work isn't the only factor in many cases of burnout. Caregiving responsibilities, financial burdens, and any other life factor that taxes your mental and emotional resources can be part of it. Even the news or social conditions may play a role. Pervasive structural racism in the United States means people of color are at greater risk for burnout because of overall heavier day-to-day burdens; and the unequal distribution of care work means women are generally at greater risk, too.

On the recommendation of a friend, I kept a weekly[3] diary during the most challenging stretch of my time at 18F, when I was chief of staff and we were under multiple cross-directed pressures. Two years later,

---

3 This was an adapted practice—my friend had kept a daily diary during her service at the USDS, but I was raising a middle-schooler and just didn't have the bandwidth to do it daily.

reading my diary entries still raises my heart rate—but at the time it was a relief and help. I would ask my husband to read it if I thought I was getting close to the edge. Your practices need to suit your own circumstances, but putting yourself in a position to reflect regularly, and having someone close to you in a position to give you a reality check, is the best way to recognize the early signs.

If you are showing the early signs of burnout, you ideally need both an urgent break and greater support. First, consider delegation—handing off some responsibilities to newer people might even be considered a service to the sustainability of your project. Then take some form of break. This can take various forms:

- Carve out a weekend, a week, or a few evenings when you set firm boundaries and don't allow work in.
- Ask your support network to show up. It's okay to ask for help with care work, housework, or other responsibilities. (It's also okay to pay for help if you can afford it.)
- Temporarily cut overtime or extra mentoring activities or committees (even though those are great) so you can have space to breathe and restore your capacities.

Act in the early stages and you will likely put yourself on a path to continue working in a way that is more sustainable for you, and therefore for your team.

CULTIVATING THE KARASS

No matter how introverted you are, please trust me when I say you don't want to do this work alone. While you will make allies, and become friends with, all kinds of partners with long backgrounds in government, you will still need the professional community of people from your core discipline. If you attended design, law, or programming-language gatherings before, don't stop now—in fact, event organizers are often very excited to showcase people doing challenging public-sector work, so consider whether you might propose a case study for a meetup or present a talk at a conference. A professional posse who can check your ideas and methods is a critical backstop, especially if people from your discipline are rare in your office. I constantly check in with other researchers about whether the adjustments I'm making to sampling and interview techniques are legit, and my inbox is always open to people who need the same.

You will also need your close people, whether they are partners, friends, family members—whoever you can call and say, "My grip on reality is slipping after this last round of meetings, help." There will be hard days, hard weeks, and hard months—they are so normal as to be commonplace, and the people you rely on will get you through. I also very strongly encourage you to seek out the company of other people doing civic tech and institutional work, whatever your background and whatever your approach.

Jake Brewer, a leading light of the civic tech community, used the phrase "cultivate the karass"—a term coined by Kurt Vonnegut for a group of people linked in a common mission, whether they know each other or not. I take this to heart and take "cultivate" to mean enrich, strengthen, challenge.

I don't know you, my reader, yet, but I know you bring something to our field that no other individual does. Someone in the community has just the piece of advice or perspective you need, and you in turn have just the perspective or skill (or even the right joke at the right moment) that someone else needs. If this is a fifty-year project, and as difficult as it feels, we all need each other.

• • •

Civic tech work has more and less intense versions. You can step up or step down your commitment as you go. But whether you're spending an evening a week or several years of your career at it, you're part of a community. And that community is working to get better at supporting its people.

In seeking support from others and sharing your obstacles, you will make more space for the community to work together to overcome them. In writing or speaking publicly or privately about the work, you will contribute to our shared understanding of the mission and the shifting ecosystem. In critiquing our community where it fails in inclusiveness, you'll give it opportunities to be better. In taking such critiques seriously and acting on them, you'll move us forward. In admitting what you don't know and holding space for others to admit it, you'll set an example that benefits the whole community.

There are many ways to be connected, and many ways to contribute as we go into our teenage years as a field. We've spent the last ten or twelve years showing what's possible, and we have some real achievements under our belt. But there is so much left to do.

We're entering the stage where we grow up and operationalize these ways of working with civic partners. It's going to be a tough road ahead, no question, but there are possibilities everywhere. The more you are connected, at whatever level of social intensity works for you, the more options you will have when you inevitably need support. And we'll all be here for you—we're in this together.

CONCLUSION

I can't thank you enough for reading this. I want to leave you with a few final thoughts about where we as a field go from here.

WHAT'S NEXT FOR CIVIC TECH?

I've described our project as a fifty-year one, with the field just now entering its teens. As a current parent of a teenager, I'm acutely aware that the teenage years are short and that if you don't learn lessons during this time, there will be much more painful ones to learn in your twenties.

Looking at this field, as I've necessarily done in the months of writing this book, I see a growing strength in practice, but still a relatively small impact compared to the scale of the institutions we hope to shift. To use my own pairing, we have done a solid job of showing what's possible, and now it's time to reflect and turn to doing what's necessary to solidify and extend these possibilities.

Given the momentous political events of the last few years, the fiction that we are not political needs to end. We can still be nonpartisan, but I believe we have a responsibility to align our civic tech work with justice and care. To do this, we need to acknowledge that this field is overly white, and lift up the voices of the underrepresented civic tech pioneers who have been saying important things for the last decade. We need to throw the doors open and welcome more people from more backgrounds, and make it easier for juniors to navigate the field. We need to make sure each of our projects acknowledges and benefits from prior work, and we need to treat policy and advocacy colleagues as full stakeholders.

From a technology and change work perspective, we need to earn our way deeper into the institutional technology "stack." We need to be helping with more algorithms and back-end systems—the metaphorical "big iron"—and taking on projects that explicitly build capacity for institutional partners. We need to tackle huge practice challenges like procurement and be unafraid to advise leaders working on those nontechnical but critical areas.

All of this is in service of the vision of public digital goods that perform as well as commercial ones for accessing services, exercising rights, and building communities. We need to engage the idea of digital public infrastructure, and better define and communicate the idea of public digital goods.

To do these things, we'll need to institutionalize a bit. We need many more books than this one, from different perspectives, and we need archives and a coherent history of projects, both failed and successful. We need more organizations that more types of people can join, and more ways to convene, whether in person or online. We need to strengthen our ability to support community members so we burn fewer people out, and we need to keep opening and improving the community we have.

I hope that when I look back on this book in 2030, we'll have a vibrant, accessible field that has earned a place as a core discipline of good government and strong institutions. And I hope many of you will be honored contributors, in ways I've barely begun to imagine.

RESOURCES

An opinionated list of things you might find directly useful in your civic tech work, and where to find more connections on your own.

Finding Civic Tech People and Projects

There's probably civic tech work going on somewhere near you—if not geographically, then definitely online. Here are some ideas to get connected to the community.

- You can find the closest volunteer civic tech group by looking up the Code for America Brigade's chapters (https://brigade.codeforamerica.org), or by searching for "open data [yourcity]" or "civic tech [yourcity]". It's also a great idea to attend community meetings in your area to find out what problems the community is grappling with.
- There's a large community on Twitter, and the hashtags #civictech and #govtech are reliable starting points. #opendata, #servicedesign, and #smartcities are broader conversations that often have civic tech content as well.

- If you're in a city with a large government digital team, check to see whether they hold regular brown bags or potlucks for the community (many do).
- If you can afford it, go to the Code for America Summit sometime. The conference is huge and can be daunting, but offers quite a few sessions and events designed to make first-time attendees comfortable.
- Civic Hall's *Civic Tech Field Guide* has an extensive, crowdsourced listing of civic tech projects globally (https://civictech.guide/).

Tools You Can Use in Your Civic Tech Work

All of these are resources you might apply directly in a project.

Tools and Standards for Digital Work

- *Digital Services Playbook* from the United States Digital Service, https://playbook.cio.gov/.
- *The Open Data Handbook* from the Open Knowledge Foundation, https://opendatahandbook.org/.
- The *United States Web Design System* (https://designsystem.digital.gov) is a free, open-source library of responsive, accessible website components that any government project can use.
- Plainlanguage.gov (https://plainlanguage.gov) is the federal government's resource on plain writing for public-sector entities.

Data on the Public's Use of the Internet

- The Pew Internet and American Life Project (https://pewinternet.org) is an indispensable regular survey of the technologies Americans use online, and the attitudes they hold about them.
- Brookings Metro's neighborhood broadband data, published in 2020, is the most granular data I know of on internet access (https://www.brookings.edu/blog/the-avenue/2020/02/05/neighborhood-broadband-data-makes-it-clear-we-need-an-agenda-to-fight-digital-poverty/).

- Find datasets published by a state or city government by going to data.[government].gov or searching for "open data [place]". The federal version is just data.gov.

Templates for Inclusion

- Project Include's guide for writing company codes of conduct: https://projectinclude.org/writing_cocs
- Plone, a long-running open-source project, has a short and strong code of conduct that many other organizations have adopted or adapted. I particularly appreciate its emphasis on community responsibility: https://plone.org/foundation/materials/foundation-resolutions/code-of-conduct.
- Cornell University's checklist for accessible physical meetings is excellent if your group meets in person: https://accessibility.cornell.edu/event-planning/accessible-meeting-and-event-checklist/.

Civic Tech Companies

There are far too many for a list, so I'll offer a few examples of companies that present themselves as part of civic tech, as a template for finding more.

Consultancies

- **Civilla** is a Detroit-based design consultancy with a focus on the public sector. These exist all over the country, and many are organized as nonprofits, B Corps, or public-benefit corporations (PBCs): https://www.civilla.com.
- **DataMade** is a consultancy that helps organizations build tools and applications for the public good using open data: https://datamade.us.
- **Nava PBC** is a consultancy founded by alumni of the HealthCare.gov rescue that focuses on digital projects for federal and state agencies. They build custom technology and maintain major sites: https://www.navapbc.com.

There are more firms focusing on this space every year. I sometimes call them "new school vendors," and they are starting to rival government digital service teams in the number of technologists they hire.

Mutual Aid and Participation Projects

- **The Human Utility** is a nonprofit company that matches donors with people with punitive water bills in distressed counties, to free them from the debt and get their water turned back on. A facilitated mutual aid model: https://detroitwaterproject.org.
- **Streetmix** is an open-source project that is free for city planners and residents to use. (It began as a side project for a few Code for America fellows and is now independently maintained with foundation sponsorship.) To date, it has been used to create more than a hundred thousand plans, and anyone can contribute on GitHub: https://streetmix.net/.

Product Companies

- **SeamlessDocs** is a venture-funded start-up that converts paper or PDF forms into web forms and helps organizations manage the data. They are optimized to sell to governments and agencies, mostly at the municipal and state level: https://seamlessdocs.com.
- **Granicus** is a company that offers enterprise-scale communications solutions for local and state governments, including meeting recording, safe email messaging, and cloud storage: https://granicus.com.
- **Esri** is an enormous geodata solutions company that has many government customers and caters to government needs: https://esri.com.

Further Places to Look:

- AngelList maintains a category for civic tech startups: https://angel.co/civic-tech-1.
- The Govtech Fund's portfolio companies are a good starting point: http://govtechfund.com/portfolio/.

Programs to Help Small Companies as Government Vendors

Health and Human Services (HHS) and the Small Business Administration (SBA) maintain a good list of these programs. Most states consider qualification for these federal programs in their procurement as well: https://www.hhs.gov/grants/small-business-programs/programs-supporting-small-businesses/index.html.

Organizations That Work to Bring Private-Sector Technologists into Government

If you want to get a job inside government with additional support from an organization that understands the transition from the private sector, these are great places to start.

- 18F is an internal federal government digital consultancy that hires people on two- to four-year terms (https://18f.gsa.gov/).
- Code for America offers a yearlong Community Fellowship, as well as permanent staff jobs working with government partners (https://www.codeforamerica.org/).
- Coding It Forward offers a Civic Digital Fellowship for college students (https://www.codingitforward.com/).
- The General Services Administration offers a twelve-month Presidential Innovation Fellows program (https://presidentialinnovationfellows.gov/).
- TechCongress offers a Congressional Digital Services Fellowship (https://www.techcongress.io/).
- United States Digital Response is a nonprofit supporting emergency technology projects, usually for shorter terms (https://www.usdigitalresponse.org/).
- United States Digital Service is an agency of the federal government that hires people on three-month to two-year terms (https://www.usds.gov/).

More Digital Service Groups

The United States Digital Service and 18F are the federal teams, but many large cities and several states (California, Colorado, Georgia, Massachusetts, New Jersey, and New York as of summer 2020) now have their own version. Try searching "[city or state] digital service" to see if your city or state has one. USDS, which is a White House office, has also spun out independent, agency-specific teams at Defense, VA, and HHS.

Academic and Other Institutions Concerned with Civic Tech

I include these because they are great places to look for partnership, events, and sometimes funding. Several offer fellowships or project grants.

- The Ash Center for Democratic Governance and Innovation at the Harvard John F. Kennedy School of Government
- The Beeck Center for Social Impact and Innovation at Georgetown University
- Bloomberg Philanthropies' What Works Cities Initiative
- The Brennan Center for Justice at New York University School of Law
- Center for Civic Design
- Ford Foundation
- The Institute for Digital Public Infrastructure at University of Massachusetts at Amherst (launching Fall 2020)
- Knight Foundation
- New America
- Omidyar Network
- OpenGov Partnership
- Sunlight Foundation

FURTHER READING

These references go deeper into topics I've discussed in this book. Some are foundational blog posts and some are obscure books; one is a national founding document. All have made me think, and helped me practice.

I've generally organized the resources in each section from light to heavy reading, starting with blog posts and summaries and building toward books, with any academic works at the end.

General References

- Mike Bracken, "On Strategy: The Strategy Is Delivery. Again," January 6, 2013, https://mikebracken.com/blog/the-strategy-is-delivery-again/.
- Matt Edgar, "Delivering Digital Service: This Much I Have Learned," *Matt Edgar Writes Here*, January 27, 2020, https://blog.mattedgar.com/2020/01/27/delivering-digital-service-this-much-i-have-learned/.

- Tim O'Reilly, "Government as a Platform," *annotations* 6, no. 1 (2010): 13–40, https://www.mitpressjournals. org/doi/pdf/10.1162/INOV_a_00056.
- Eric Gordon and Rogelio Alejandro Lopez, "The Practice of Civic Tech: Tensions in the Adoption and Use of New Technologies in Community Based Organizations," *Media and Communication* 7, no. 3 (2019), https://www.cogitatiopress.com/ mediaandcommunication/article/view/2180. Goes into depth about technology and community-based organizations.
- Amanda Clarke, "Digital Government Units: What Are They, and What Do They Mean for Digital Era Public Management Renewal?," *International Public Management Journal* 23, no. 3 (2020): 358–379, https://doi.org/10.1080/10967494.2019.16 86447. Examines national digital teams in English-speaking countries around the world and discusses how to assess their effectiveness from a public administration perspective.
- Hana Schank and Sarah Hudson, *The Government Fix* (Sense & Respond Press, 2019).
- Brett Goldstein and Lauren Dyson, eds., *Beyond Transparency: Open Data and the Future of Civic Innovation* by Code for America (Code for America Press, 2013), https://beyondtransparency. org/part-2/pioneering-open-data-standards-the-gtfs-story/.
- Andrew Schrock, Civic Tech (Long Beach, CA: Rogue Academic Press, 2018).

Big Ideas

- The Constitution of the United States. (I'm not kidding—when was the last time you read it?) The government keeps a nicely indexed copy online at the National Archives (https://www.archives.gov/founding-docs/constitution-transcript) or you can order a pocket version as a booklet from several publishers. (Search for "pocket constitution".)
- Atul Gawande, "Slow Ideas," *New Yorker*, July 29, 2013, https:// www.newyorker.com/magazine/2013/07/29/slow-ideas.

- Ethan Zuckerman, "The Case for Digital Public Infrastructure," Knight First Amendment Institute, Columbia University, January 17, 2020, https://knightcolumbia.org/content/the-case-for-digital-public-infrastructure.

Resources for Inclusive Tech and Anti-Racism

- Reginé M. Gilbert, *Inclusive Design for a Digital World: Designing with Accessibility in Mind* (Berkeley: University of California Press, 2019).
- Sarah Horton and Whitney Quesenbery, *A Web for Everyone: Designing Accessible User Experiences* (Brooklyn, NY: Rosenfeld Media, 2014).
- Ijeoma Oluo, *So You Want to Talk about Race* (New York: Seal Press, 2018).
- Ibram X Kendi, *How to Be an Anti-Racist* (New York: One World, 2019).
- Alice Wong, ed., *Disability Visibility: First-Person Stories from the Twenty-First Century* (New York: Vintage Books, 2020).
- Christina Dunbar-Hester, *Hacking Diversity: The Politics of Inclusion in Open Technology Cultures* (Princeton: Princeton University Press, 2019).

Cautions for Civic Tech

It's important to keep asking whether we're actually doing good. Here are a few readings that have helped me ask that question in new ways.

- Rachel Coldicutt, "Inside the Clubcard Panopticon: Why Dominic Cummings' Seeing Room Might Not See All That Much," *The Startup*, Medium, January 10, 2020, https://medium.com/swlh/inside-the-clubcard-panopticon-why-dominic-cummings-seeing-room-might-not-see-all-that-much-f940a48ae1cd.
- Joshua Tauberer, "So You Want to Reform Democracy," *Civic Tech Thoughts from JoshData*, Medium, November 22, 2015, https://medium.com/civic-tech-thoughts-from-joshdata/so-you-want-to-reform-democracy-7f3b1ef10597.

- Russell Davies, "Death to Innovation," October 2, 2013, https://russelldavies.typepad.com/planning/2013/10/death-to-innovation.html.
- Virginia Eubanks, *Automating Inequality: How High-Tech Tools Profile, Police, and Punish the Poor* (New York: Picador, 2018). For a good summary interview, see Jenn Stroud Rossmann, "Public Thinker: Virginia Eubanks on Digital Surveillance and People Power," *Public Books*, July 9, 2020, https://www.publicbooks.org/public-thinker-virginia-eubanks-on-digital-surveillance-and-people-power/.
- James C. Scott, *Seeing Like A State: How Certain Schemes to Improve the Human Condition Have Failed* (New Haven: Yale University Press, 1998).

Discipline Resources with a Public-Sector Angle

- **Product Management**

  » Nikki Lee and Karla Reinsel, "Building Product Management Capacity in Government, Part 1," 18F, August 22, 2019, https://18f.gsa.gov/2019/08/22/building-product-management-capacity-in-government-part-1/.

  » Scott Colfer, Product Management Handbook (2018), https://scottcolfer.com/product-management-handbook/.

- **Design and Research**

  » United Kingdom Government Digital Service, "Government Design Principles," GOV.UK, April 3, 2012, https://www.gov.uk/guidance/government-design-principles.

  » Bernard Tyers, "Doing Ethical Research with Vulnerable Users," ei8fdb.org, July 2, 2019, http://www.ei8fdb.org/thoughts/2019/07/doing-ethical-research-with-vulnerable-users/.

  » Creative Reaction Lab, *Field Guide: Equity-Centered Community Design*, https://www.creativereactionlab.com/store/field-guide-equity-centered-community-design.

» Daniel X. O'Neil and the Smart Chicago Collaborative, *The CUTgroup Book* (2017), https://irp-cdn.multiscreensite.com/9614ecbe/files/uploaded/TheCUTGroupBook.pdf.

» Lou Downe, *Good Services: How to Design Services That Work* (Amsterdam: BIS Publishers, 2020).

» Sasha Costanza-Chock, *Design Justice: Community-Led Practices to Build the Worlds We Need* (Cambridge, MA: MIT Press, 2020).

» Elizabeth Buie and Dianne Murray, eds., *Usability in Government Systems: User Experience Design for Citizens and Public Servants* (San Francisco: Morgan Kaufmann, 2012).

- **Engineering**

This isn't my area of expertise, but people I trust have cited some of these as helpful to their own practice.

» Marianne Bellotti, "Is COBOL Holding You Hostage with Math?," *Programming*, Medium, July 28, 2018, https://medium.com/@bellmar/is-cobol-holding-you-hostage-with-math-5498c0eb428b.

» Joshua Tauberer, *Open Government Data: The Book* (2014), https://opengovdata.io.

» Ben Frain, *Enduring CSS* (Birmingham, UK: Packt Publishing, 2017).

» Sam Newman, *Monolith to Microservices* (Sebastopol, CA: O'Reilly Media, 2019).

- **Policy**

» Alex Soble and Mike Gintz, "Rapid Implementation of Policy as Code," 18F, May 12, 2020, https://18f.gsa.gov/2020/05/12/rapid-implementation-of-policy-as-code/.

» Jennifer Pahlka, "Delivery-Driven Policy: Policy Designed for the Digital Age," Code for America, November 5, 2019, https://www.codeforamerica.org/news/delivery-driven-policy.

» Xun Wu et al., *The Public Policy Primer* (London: Routledge, 2010).

- **Soft Skills**
  - » Tom Critchlow, "Navigating Power & Status: How to Get Things Done inside Organizations by Understanding Power Potholes and Status Switching," June 24, 2020, https://tomcritchlow.com/2020/06/24/navigating-power-status/.
  - » Josh Gee, "What I Learned in Two Years of Moving Government Forms Online," Medium, February 22, 2018, https://medium.com/@jgee/what-i-learned-in-two-years-of-moving-government-forms-online-1edc4c2aa089.

- **Government Budgets**
  - » "Policy Basics: Introduction to the Federal Budget Process," Center on Budget and Policy Priorities, April 2, 2020, https://www.cbpp.org/research/policy-basics-introduction-to-the-federal-budget-process (Ch 4).
  - » Bruce A. Wallin, "Budget Processes, State," Urban Institute, n.d. , https://www.urban.org/sites/default/files/publication/71026/1000518-Budget-Processes-State.PDF.
  - » "Public Budgets," National League of Cities, n.d., https://bit.ly/ACTPG-1.

Resources for Government That May Also Be Useful to Civic Technologists

- Mark Headd, How to Talk to Civic Hackers, https://www.civichacking.guide/. An online book for government folks who want to work with techies. It's an interesting perspective to read in parallel with this book.
- Robin Carnahan, Randy Hart, and Waldo Jaquith, *De-risking Custom Technology Projects: A Handbook for State Grantee Budgeting and Oversight* (August 5, 2019), https://github.com/18F/technology-budgeting/blob/master/handbook.md. Gets into depth on procurement issues at the state level.

ACKNOWLEDGMENTS

While I'm self-publishing this book, I most certainly didn't create it alone. Many people inside and outside of civic tech have provided encouragement, corrections, and material help. And the paperback form of *A Civic Technologist's Practice Guide* wouldn't exist without a project completion grant from the Beeck Center for Social Impact + Innovation at Georgetown University and its Digital Service Collaborative funded by The Rockefeller Foundation. I'm grateful for their generous support.

The first people I told about this idea were Dana Chisnell and my former leadership teammates at 18F, Rebecca Piazza, Sarah Milstein and Joshua Bailes. They all kindly said "heck yes, you should do that" and it's hard to overstate how important that early encouragement is for a project like this. As I got started, I asked a large group of former colleagues and respected friends to check my work, and I'd like to thank Dana, Josh, Lane Becker, Tiffani Ashley Bell, Ron Bronson, Alan Brouilette, Eddie Fernández, Sha Hwang, Nikki Lee, Jack Madans, Jennifer Pahlka, Angelica Quicksey, Alex Soble, and Cori Zarek for reading chapters and entire drafts with a critical eye. Any errors that made it past this formidably knowledgeable group are mine alone.

I'm also indebted to Lane and to Randy Hart for conversations about procurement, and to Alex and to Sasha Magee for helping me figure out how to talk about language flexibility for engineers. Midway through the editing process, my father, Stevan Harrell, asked to read the book, and he provided both an outsider's view of this introduction to civic tech and an experienced author's take on the process - thanks, Dad!

My kind and indefatigable editor, Sally Kerrigan, was the best possible partner for turning an extended brain dump into a usable book. And Lisa Maria Marquis, who introduced me to Sally, deserves my thanks as well. As copy editor, Caren Litherland sorted out my inconsistencies and made the writing sound like me, only better. I'm grateful to Scott Berkun, Sam Ladner, Mike Monteiro, Kat Vellos, and MK Williams for advice and help on self-publishing. And the wonderful team at Oxide Design hit my brief of "a geeky survival manual in the American civic design tradition" out of the park.

No one writes a book without substantial support in other life arenas, especially during a pandemic. My professional coach, Samantha Soma, was an essential sounding board about a career choice I had to make to do this. And my crew of working-mom girlfriends, Jessica Gregg, Angela Ingenito, and Amanda Moore, were a lifeline this year as we traded flour for rice and commiserated about online school. I will also shout out my longtime UX research friend Erika Hall, for the pre-holiday coffee conversation that provided the spark for this whole project.

Finally, my own little family. When I got home from coffee with Erika with an outline I had written on my phone in a taxi, my other half, Jason Douglas, said not only, "of course you should do this," but, "you should do this right now, and publish it before the November election." He and our daughter, Audrey, have been not only unfailingly encouraging but enormously patient with me being on a laptop during family movie nights, working through weekends, and staring into space even more than usual. Thanks loves - you're the absolute best!

ABOUT THE AUTHOR

Cyd Harrell is a UX researcher and product manager who got hooked on civic tech at early 2010s hackathons. When Facebook bought her employer in 2012, she chose to invest her career in public service technology work. Cyd has helped US city, county, federal, and state agencies unlock the power of technology to serve constituents. She has worked independently, with the Center for Civic Design, Code for America, and 18F. Over the years, Cyd has been a mentor and leader to many people in the field, and she is proud to have served as the first chief of staff of 18F. She is dedicated to a more inclusive, more capable, and better coordinated civic tech movement. Cyd lives in San Francisco with her husband and daughter. She is easy to find on Twitter and always happy to talk to civic technologists.

CPSIA information can be obtained
at www.ICGtesting.com
Printed in the USA
FSHW011807011021